DAILY LIFE DURING THE INDIAN MUTINY

DAILY LIFE DURING THE INDIAN MUTINY

PERSONAL EXPERIENCES OF 1857

J. W. SHERER, C. S. I.

GYAN

Published by

GYAN

Gyan Publishing House
5, Ansari Road
Daryaganj, New Delhi-110002
Phone: 011-47034999, 9811692060
E-mail: books@gyanbooks.com

Distribution Network
gyanbooks.com
India, USA, Canada, UK, Australia, France

ISBN: 978-81-212-9330-3 (PB)
First Published, 1898

2nd Impression 2023

Printed at: Gyan Press, Delhi.

DAILY LIFE DURING THE INDIAN MUTINY

AUTHOR: J. W. SHERER

From a photograph by Owen of Bournemouth.

Faithfully yours
J. W. Sherer

DAILY LIFE DURING THE INDIAN MUTINY

PERSONAL EXPERIENCES OF 1857

BY

J. W. SHERER, C.S.I.

"ἔνθ' ἄριστοι
ἔσχον πολέμοιο νεῖκος ἐσχάταις ἐλπίσιν"
—*Pindar*

Where our best
Sustained the strife of war
When hopes were at their lowest

LONDON
SWAN SONNENSCHEIN & CO., LTD.
PATERNOSTER SQUARE
1898

DAILY LIFE DURING THE MUTINY

INTRODUCTION

I LANDED in Calcutta in December, 1846, and after a rather long stay in connection with passing the college, finally proceeded up country in the spring of 1848, and reaching Agra, was appointed Assistant Magistrate there. In the same year, I was transferred to Muttra, where I acted as Joint-Magistrate.

In 1850, the Lieut.-Governor, Mr. James Thomason, whose father had been an intimate friend of mine, appointed me Assistant Secretary to his Government. Afterwards I acted as Registrar of the old Sudder Court, and later, became Joint-Magistrate of Allygurh.

In the cold weather of 1856, I was directed by the Revenue Board to report on the condition of lands bordering the Jumna Canals, which had suffered very much from a saline efflorescence called by the natives *Reh.* My tour led me to Paneeput, and Kurnal, and Rohtuk, and Nujufgurh, and other places, afterwards so often mentioned in accounts of the Siege of Delhi.

In Delhi itself, I staid a day or two on my way back, and particularly remember one Sunday afternoon. I went to evening prayers at the church built by Col. Skinner.

Service was, I think, at five. I must mention that, personally, I had not the slightest idea that there were any symptoms of approaching disturbance in the country, or of uneasy feeling in the Army. The function proceeded till it was time for the sermon, when, instead of going into the pulpit, Chaplain Jennings walked down the church to the font, where he commenced the celebration of a baptism. As he passed the pew, I thought I noticed a rather dogged expression on his face, as of one who should say, "I know this is a little burdensome, but I think it correct, and you must bear it." Afterwards, when the pulpit was reached, it was growing dark, and soon a candle had to be sent for. This slender, solitary light in the darkening church, and the loud voice proceeding from a figure partially occupying the small disk of brightness, had a most singular effect. The sermon, which the preacher would not curtail by a syllable on account of the lateness, dwelt, as far as I remember, on the vicissitudes of life, and urged how unwise the postponement of repentance was in the face of the absolute uncertainty of the future. I felt at the time a most unaccountable sinking of spirits; and when afterwards I came to remember how many were present, shrouded in the gloom, whose lives were rapidly drawing to a close, I grew to associate with the scene some sense of forewarning, from which my memory is now unable to disengage itself.

When the tour was over, I went to the house of my father-in-law, Harington, at Agra, to write my report. He was a judge of the old Sudder Court, and lived in the Kandaharee Bagh, an ancient tomb adapted to household purposes, and standing in a walled garden. It was in this, walking with him and a colonel of native infantry, that the possibility of a mutiny first struck me. The subject of the cartridges—quite new to me—was being discussed, and the colonel said if the materials for greasing them were such as suspected, and biting them was insisted upon, the Sepoys would certainly not obey orders. "And," he added, "though John Sepoy seems such a quiet fellow in the lines, on such matters as his caste, his religion, or his women, if he gets off his head, there is no violence or cruelty he would not commit." Thus was the seed sown in one's mind of much subsequent anxiety.

During my stay at Agra, Wulleedad Khan, who afterwards gave much trouble at his own town, Boolundshuhr, got an introduction to me, and called two or three times. He was then as was known afterwards, plotting against our Government amongst the Mahomedans of Agra, and I suppose made up to me in the hopes of hearing from me what Harington and men in his position thought of the crisis. I remember one day saying that the misapprehension in the Army was very extraordinary, and Wulleedad answered, "But it is of no importance. What could revolted Sepoys do? A soldier untrue to his salt is not a formidable enemy." When we finally parted, he said he hoped sooner or later the Government (Sircar) would send me to Boolundshuhr. It is very odd he should have taken the trouble to talk in this false way. I can only suppose he wished to create a favourable impression of loyalty, as a string to his bow in case of accidents.

My report was approved of by the new Lieut.-Governor, Mr. John Colvin, and he appointed me to act as Magistrate and Collector of Futtehpore-Hussowa, a district situated in the Doab, between Cawnpore and Allahabad. The township of Futtehpore itself was on the Grand Trunk Road, and is now a railway station about 35 miles from Cawnpore I travelled towards my new home, with my wife and children, in two posting carriages, and as it was getting very hot we moved at night, being drawn by coolies along the smooth road. We constantly passed groups of Sepoys, leave having been purposely given with exceptional freedom. The Magistrate of Cawnpore, Mr. Hillersdon, had asked us to put up with him, and we stayed a day or two in his comfortable bungalow in Nuwab Gunj. Mrs. Hillersdon was an accomplished pianist—a favourite pupil of Ascher—and she delighted us with some charming music, both on her own instrument and on the concertina, which, in her hands, proved itself as satisfactory as it usually is very much the contrary with less skilful players. She was fond of Mendelssohn's *Rondo Capriccios*, then not hackneyed, and I never hear the piece without recollections of the still interior of the Cawnpore house, its accomplished mistress, her husband, her children, her brother-in-law—Col. Hillersdon—all doomed to speedy and painful destruction. Little did I think, as I sat talking with Hillersdon over friends we had both known at Muttra, that in a month or two I should be his successor, and that four only would be alive of all our countrymen whose duties had collected them at Cawnpore, and of the families that had gathered around them.

When we reached our destination, we found much excitement, but no special knowledge of the state of affairs at Allahabad, further than that the 6th Regiment of Native Infantry was considered shaky. As the treasury guard at Futtehpore, commanded by a Subahdar, was supplied by that regiment, its conduct was of local interest. I relieved my predecessor, Mr. Edmonstone, and he went off to Allahabad, and then the circle at the station consisted of four railway engineers engaged in constructing the new line to Cawnpore, *viz.*, Bews, Oswin, Heathcote, and a fourth whose name has escaped me. Then there was Mr. Robert Tucker, the judge, and Elliott Macnaghten, Assistant Magistrate, and Dr. Hutchinson and his wife, and Anderson, opium agent, and his mother, and a salt inspector who was often away in the district, and ourselves.

Our judge was a tall, large-boned man, eccentric in some of his views, but of an exceedingly fine character. He was one of those of whom you felt absolutely certain that in no circumstances of life, however trying, would any unworthy motive ever even cross his mind. He was possessed of much information, and conversed with an easy flow of language, and in a voice of full and pleasant tone, so that it was an enjoyment to listen to him. Though vivacious and social enough, his life was directed by strict principles of what old Isaak Walton called "the primitive piety." In the court, where he sat at the daily task, he had had painted on the wall over his chair a label with these words, "Thou God seest me." At the entry of the town, too, he had got permission to erect pillars by the wayside, on which he had had inscribed, in the vernacular, the Ten Commandments, and sundry religious precepts.

Though there was no immediate cause for apprehension, I received orders not to let the ladies stay in case of threatened danger. The mail-carts seemed to afford a fair test of general security, and as long as they ran regularly both ways, I did not think any action necessary. But at last, one night, there was no mail from the westward. A sowar usually came up at midnight with the letters, and I was awakened to see if there was any news of importance. On this occasion he waited an hour or two, and then rode up to say the cart had not arrived. My brother-in-law, Forbes, who had been ordered home sick, was staying with us, and his wife and children were with him. I had to give notice in the morning that unless the mail-cart came at noon, there must be a start for Allahabad. Twelve struck, no mail-cart. So the posting carriages were sent for, and the two families, under the protection of Forbes, were sent off. When they reached Allahabad, the road to Calcutta was reported open, and they pushed on; and the last day there was any post from Allahabad, there came a mere scrap of untidy paper with the words "all safe" written on it, and the Calcutta post-mark.

The same day my people left me, I warned the other ladies; and as they were more or less expecting an intimation, their arrangements were complete, and off they went.

As it happened, the mail-cart had only broken down, and at last came in; but affairs were very gloomy, and it was a great relief to know that no one was left but those whose duties required them to stay. All Eurasians connected with the offices decided on such plans for the safety of their families as seemed to them the most suitable. I occupied a large and roomy house, which had been built by my predecessor, and as it seemed most desirable that we should act together in case of emergency, I proposed to all the men that we should make a common home of the only place in the station that would accommodate so large a party.

The news grew worse. English soldiers, by twos and threes, occasionally passed through towards Cawnpore in conveyances, and these the Kotwal, or head constable of the town, who was really a rebel in the guise of a humourist, called the *choontee fouj*, or ant-army. One evening three officers called on us on their way westward. One was named Bax, and another was a young fellow just joining, and we made them stay supper. Afterwards a song or two followed, and they left us at midnight, not without "one cheer more," and so departed—to their fate. The railway men tried to work in the mornings, but could not manage much; and though our courts and office were open, yet there was no business. Only the opium-eaters were constant; they came at the stated hour for their supply of the drug. They dwelt in dreamland, and were not interested in the troubles of real life. The sub-officers out in the district reported that crime had ceased altogether.

A Sanscrit poet describes how, in an overwhelmingly hot season, the cobra lay under the peacock's wing, and the frog, again, reclined beneath the hood of the cobra. All antipathies and antagonisms were forgotten. And so, amongst the peasantry around us, there was a general expectation which paralysed all activity. The thief sat down by the door-keeper, and the bad characters sought the shelter of the miser's wall; all were waiting—waiting—they certainly had no idea for what.

We had had the celebrated "chupatties" in our district; but I am almost inclined to think more has been made of them than was their due. The village watchmen received them, and forwarded them, or similar ones, elsewhere, as they were requested to do; but all agree that the watchmen had no definite idea of what was meant. If the transmission of these cakes was only intended to create a mysterious uneasiness, that object was gained. But if the affair was a signal for united action, it failed altogether, and ended in a bungle, for no united action took place. And it must be remembered that the circulation of chupatties is a superstitious practice not unknown in Central India, resorted to, we are told, in the hope of passing on epidemics.

When I was leaving Agra, the Government Secretary, knowing that I had little or no experience in managing a district, kindly told me of the Mahomedan Deputy-Collector, Hikmut-Oollah, at Futtehpore, and recommended me to lean on him as a man of complete acquaintance with that part of the country, intelligent, tried, and entirely to be trusted. As soon as I arrived, he, of course, came to see me, and I found him tall, but with rather a stooping, invalid figure, of pale, olive complexion, and with reticent eyes—eyes, that is, from which he withheld all expression, till he could form some idea of my character. He had the grave, graceful manners of his race; but the impression he produced on my mind was that of a person astute rather than frank, and whose behaviour would be coloured by his opinion of his official superior. Somehow, he reminded me of the Italian secretaries one sees in a picture gallery, with their black velvet doublets and delicate lace collars, and their calm, mask-like faces.

During the ominously tranquil time I have described—tranquil, indeed, only in our immediate neighbourhood, for the administration was breaking down in all directions—the Deputy-Collector hardly ever came near me. When he did, and the conversation turned on the state of the army, he affected to ignore any serious danger from Sepoys without discipline, and alienated from their lawful leaders. This was exactly the tone of Wulleedad Khan. But the daily report from the treasury was kept up as usual. Generally the Subahdar came himself. He was a Brahmin, and though I naturally expressed no doubt of his fidelity, he seemed particularly anxious to impress upon me that I might entirely trust him. Indeed, one morning he rose from his seat abruptly, opened his coat, and drew out his sacrificial thread, and holding it up in his hand, he exclaimed in a strong voice, "If I am not faithful to the Government (Sircar), Collector Sahib, may Gunga strike me dead!" But when the Subahdar did not come in person, a slight, pleasant-faced old Jemadar took his place, and I could plainly see that *his* mind was greatly distressed. His heart was not in the mischief, and yet he dared not make any disclosures. He spoke in a mournful voice, and always asked what the news was from Allahabad. Once in answer to my question, "Well, are your men still quite in hand?" "Oh, yes," he said, "all is right." And then, after a short pause, he added, "But the young are obstinate, and if they get the wind into their heads, they won't listen to advice." But though he thus indicated that things were not what could be wished, he would go no further. I think he was afraid if he told me anything definite, I might ask the Subahdar if it was true.

At last an afternoon came which was cloudy and overcast, and after luncheon, we opened the windows and venetian blinds towards the west, and sat out in the verandah. There was a purple haze over the distance, and a sound of guns was distinctly heard. The firing had been going on since mid-day, but we had not known of it in the muffled house; and every now and then the deep rumble of heavy ordnance came rolling over the fields. We were witnesses, through our hearing, of an historical event, for the Nana was attacking Wheeler's entrenchment for the first time. The day was, therefore, June 6th. The Sub-Collector, posted half-way to Cawnpore, had been told to write all intelligence he could gather, and that evening a letter arrived from him, full of extravagance. "What Roostums were these, who, a mere handful, were resisting hordes of their enemies? What courage! what resource! The pen refused to proceed, and bowed itself down before qualities which it would require a Furdoosee to rightly celebrate." This rodomontade had to us a significance all its own. The storm was close upon us.

I begin my narrative as I began it in the "Memories," but hope that this Introduction will render it less abrupt. In the last few paragraphs, I have a little anticipated events; but I do not think any confusion will arise.

I

WITHDRAWAL

Well, then, there we were—all the men of the station, collected in the large house at Futtehpore which had been built by the last Collector. Each day our movements became more restricted. We generally drove in the evening, and one of the railwaymen had a tandem. This practice had to be given up. Then a day or two before the finale we heard that a party of the 2nd Cavalry, who had taken treasure to Allahabad, would be returning, and that their passage through the place might be the signal for a disturbance; and it was rumoured they would perhaps join the treasury guard, and assist in removing the money. We had begun to sleep on the roof of the house, which roof was a rambling place, but approached only by a ladder, at the top of which was a door capable of being fastened. But in prospect of an outbreak of any sort, it seemed as well, this morning of the expected transit, to retain our position on the roof during the day also. The Subahdar had sent word that perfect reliance was to be placed in him, and that if the Cavalry attempted to come near the treasury he would fire into them forthwith. A Zemindar had kindly placed a number of matchlock-men at our disposal, and I sent word to the Subahdar to say that these men would be stationed in a garden not far from our gate; that they had received instructions not to assume the offensive, but to let the

Cavalry pass; then, if they heard firing at the treasury, to move on and take the Cavalry in the rear. This the man in charge of them promised to do. It seemed undesirable that any of our little garrison should take part with the matchlock men, because of their fidelity there seemed no guarantee whatever. From our roof we all watched the proceedings with the greatest interest. If we saw any of the Cavalry they could only have seemed like distant forms moving behind the trees. The sound of hoofs, however, was distinct. They passed the garden, where the matchlocks were, at a trot, and then there was a halt; and as we afterwards learnt, one or two men were sent to parley at the treasury.

Again we heard the sound of hoofs, and soon after a messenger came to say that the Cavalry had gone on to Cawnpore. It seemed right that the Subahdar should have credit for the result, whether accidental or not. So Macnaghten, the assistant magistrate, and I rode down to the guard. All the Sepoys had their muskets, and the Subahdar was in a glow of self-satisfaction, as he ordered us seats, and exclaimed: "I told you there was no cause for apprehension." It seems that some zealous Mahomedans had gone out of the town to meet the Cavalry, and to tell them to beware of an ambush which the English had laid for them in a garden adjoining the road. They rode out of the street, therefore, in the greatest trepidation, and if they ever intended coming to the treasury, gave up the idea, and sent an embassy to the guard, with whom, however, the Subahdar refused to treat. Things cleared a little for that day, and we dined below. It occurred to us, however, that the punkahs were sources of danger, because, if they had been set on fire, the rafters would have caught, and our stronghold, the roof, have become untenable. So, when dinner was over we cut all the punkahs down and brought them outside. Some thoughtless tongue said: "Let us burn them!" and the suggestion was immediately carried out. The wretched things were as dry as tinder, and flared up in a most prodigious way. So great a blaze would create alarm in the town, and attract the most unnecessary attention; but what could we do? The fire was easy enough to light, but impossible to extinguish; so we could only wait,—our anxious faces lighted up with the brazen glare. In the midst of the unwelcome illumination, a peasant arrived, breathless with terror, and said there was a body of Cavalry in the next field. We withdrew to the roof, but the horsemen passed away. They belonged, we were told, to an Irregular regiment, and were desirous of moving westward without adventures.

Next day was a morning of troubles. News was brought that the mass of convicts had been let loose at Allahabad, and that numbers were entering our district. The peasantry, too, were getting unsteady. Groups of them were seen wandering towards the station, and, we soon heard, were carrying off doors and wood or iron work of any description they could get possession of, from the unoccupied bungalows. Sinister reports also came that our jail was in danger. The Darogha was in communication with the Subahdar as to whether he should release the prisoners, and the Subahdar was favourable to the proposition, thinking, probably, that if they broke out they might give trouble about the treasure, but would disperse if merely dismissed. We knew that the 6th N.I. had gone at Allahabad, and were certain the party at Futtehpore was only meditating how the booty could be got away. Early in the afternoon we saw from the roof a great number of people approaching from the city. They gradually advanced to our gate, and then the main body stopped, and one or two men came forward. I say we saw, meaning those who were on watch saw, for individually, feeling the great heat, I had fallen asleep in one of the dark, spacious rooms within. It was announced that the Deputy-Collector wished to speak to me; and, going out, I found my Italian Secretary friend with a sword, and an assumed warlike look scarcely suiting him. He introduced one or two Mussulmans with guns in their hands.

He told me that things were getting very awkward, that there was a growing disposition to disregard authority, and that under these circumstances the principal Mahomedans had armed themselves and their retainers, and were prepared to keep the public peace as far as they could;—that they had come up to pay their respects to the English authorities, and that nothing but necessity would have caused them to take the law into their own hands. He added that our presence was a great source of irritation, and that if we withdrew for a time he thought the excitement would go down. As for our attempting at present to support the British Government, it was altogether out of the question. I said in reply that we were quite willing to credit himself and his friends with loyalty, or at any rate with the absence of any hostile intentions, till we had reason to think otherwise; that, with regard to our movements, they were undecided; but that should any at ergency occur I should rely on Mahomedan assistance in keeping order. As he was turning away I said to him privately: "If I go, it will only be for a month's leave." He laughed and replied: "In that case, we shall meet again." We did meet again; he in the dock, I in the witness-box.

There was one more day—June the 9th, as I take it. All the forenoon we saw the peasantry rushing about the fields. It gave the idea of a *Jacquerie*—an agricultural tumult with immense excitement but no defined object. The railway engineer of the name of Bews lived within sight of the roof, and though he had his things mostly with him, yet furniture and some closed boxes were left over at his place, and he beheld with anguish swarms of dark figures hovering round his dwelling. He was very anxious to know the law on the subject. "I have no authority, of course," he said; "but if a man comes into my house, I suppose I may prevent him taking my property?" It was held that he had a perfect right to defend his goods, and so, taking his chum with him, he rode off, armed, into the thick of the fray. It was, however, of no use. The peasants fled before him and his friend; but their numbers were so great that, as he cleared one side of the house, they over-ran the other, and his labours were wholly in vain. It has been mentioned that the subject of a withdrawal across the Jumna had been discussed by the Judge and myself, and had always met with disapproval from him. Not that he had the slightest belief in our being able to hold out; but he thought that the move should be made in the direction of Delhi, and that the gallant Subahdar and his men would escort us till we could join our countrymen in the North. The forenoon was naturally one of anxious thought. Cawnpore, Allahabad, and Rai Bareilly just over the Ganges, were all lost for the present. Should Banda go, or even that portion of the district of Banda adjoining Futtehpore, we should be completely caught in a trap. As for saving the treasure, it had really passed out of our custody into that of the Subahdar, and our presence in the district was not contributing in any way to order, or to the protection of life and property. The question was—stay and meet the chances of a very hopeless future, or go, whilst the road is still open, and join the fortunes of our comrades in the next district of Banda? I do not pretend for a moment that the natural love of new adventures, and the equally natural dislike of being cooped up in a hole, had nothing to say to our decision. But looking back upon it, after a long term of years, it seems to me a proper decision—dictated by common sense, and not blemished in any way by unworthy motives. Our plans, then, were fixed and agreed upon after debate, by all except the Judge, whose house was near the guard, and who slept amongst the Sepoys, but often came to meals with us.

However, that evening, at five o'clock, I got hold of him, and we walked up and down in a little plot grown with oleander, vinca rosea, and so on. He knew my views perfectly, and therefore I had only to tell him that we considered the emergency had now arisen. I had been informed that the jail would positively be thrown open the next morning, and, from what had been reported about the Subahdar, there could be little doubt that he was only waiting to throw off the mask. The Judge said that he himself had heard some disloyal language at night; he thought the younger Sepoys were excited, but would obey their officer, and that he was staunch. He had a great idea we should be insulted if we passed through native States as fugitives from a falling empire. Restoration—if restoration was to come at all—would spring out of Delhi, and that was the rendezvous. To a certain extent he was right. But to talk of going to Delhi and to get there were different things. I told him our plans, mentioned that we had determined to leave late that night for Banda, and entreated him to join us. But this he positively refused to do, and would not even stay dinner, but made up his mind to go home. He shook me by the hand, wished every success to our adventure, said he hoped himself to be soon on the road to Delhi, and we parted, to meet no more in this world. As this is the most painful recollection which I retain in my mind, I am anxious to dismiss it; but, upon doing so, will simply relate what occurred to this ill-fated gentleman. The sources of information are reliable, and the account of the Judge's end may be received as authentic. He returned to his house from the guard next morning early, and perhaps in the night had heard some expressions which set the question of the disloyalty of the Sepoys at rest, for he at once sent word to the Deputy-Collector (the Italian Secretary) that he wished to go to Banda, could he assist about horses for the journey? The person thus applied to sent back a message that it was not in his power to offer any assistance. It seems likely, as our jail was opened that morning, that the roads were pretty full of rough characters. The Judge mounted his horse, with his rifle slung behind him, and proceeded into the town. Perhaps he intended to call personally on the Deputy-Collector. I think it probable, however, that by that time there was considerable excitement amongst the lower Mahomedans, and that he met with some contumely, if he was not even attacked. That he used his rifle several times there is no question; and he was not the man to do so except in circumstances demanding such an extreme measure. Then he returned home and ascended to the roof of his office, a convenient oblong space which he had often said was suitable for defence. Here he spent some time, till a large body of men were seen advancing from the town. They had banners and symbols typical of the Moslem Faith, and a copy of the Koran was carried open before one of the number. They advanced to a space beneath the Judge's office, and several fire-arms were discharged towards the gaunt figure standing against the sky, deadened in its colour by the heat. There was a sharp return from the roof. Again a silence, broken only by the monotonously-muttered passages from the Koran. Again a discharge. And struck by a bullet in the forehead, Robert Tucker sank to rise no more. Thus a brave, unselfish, honourable, and nobly aspiring man passed away from earth. An excellent person, the late Dr. Duff, with no wish, I am sure, to cause pain to others, publicly wrote that Tucker *alone* fell at the post of duty. It was not so. He, in staying with the Sepoys, we, in going to new fields of action, each thought we were doing the thing that should be done. That point does not trouble me. I sometimes think that as we were several—and the Judge was one—we should have tried to oblige him to come with us. I trust the delicacy of the situation will excuse us in the eyes of good men, if there was here any failure of decision.[1]

[1] In the "Kaye-Malleson History," affairs at Futtehpore are not

The faithful Badul Khan, a table attendant who had been with me from the first, prepared us a more than usually careful dinner that night. He was not coming with us, nor indeed were any of our servants, except the syces or grooms. They were anxious, as they might well be, about their families, and their trifling goods and chattels, and leaving the Doab seemed like emigration from their own country. We can only, any of us, relate our own experiences in such matters, but I have not the slightest ingratitude to complain of in the case of native servants. They knew of our going, expressed the warmest wishes for our prosperous journey, and the hope that we should all soon meet happily again. I scarcely like to think of the dressing that night before dinner, and putting on suitable clothes should a prolonged absence from the washerman take place. It was more like being sent to school by one's mother than anything else. For my two Hindoo servants from Muttra were forestalling every contingency. One small bag was taken, but elaborate instructions were given as to where the little knick-knacks of the toilet could be found. "If I put my hand in one corner there would be a

---

quite correctly narrated. Small blame, indeed, to the authors of a work where details are so prodigiously numerous. Sir T. J. Metcalfe was never with us at Futtehpore; he was, of course, at Delhi. Such mistakes do not matter. But one statement I must notice. At p. 76, vol. vi. (new edition, 1897), this passage occurs:—

"Futtehpore was subsequently the battle-ground whereon Havelock, three days after the death of Mr. Tucker, defeated the troops of Nana Sahib."

Mr. Tucker was killed on the 10th of June, and General Havelock entered Futtehpore on the 12th of July.

This is of importance, because, if Mr. Tucker could remain in safety at Futtehpore, we ought not to have left. But, in fact, Mr. Tucker's death took place before we reached Banda.

comb, and down in another was the shoe-horn,"—and when it came at last to my saying "That will do, it is dinner time now," they both knelt down, clasped me round the knees, and wept like children, and to speak the truth, I had a good cry myself; short, sharp, relieving, and unwitnessed by the scornful. With a view to detaching little articles likely to excite cupidity, I gave a large gold seal of my father's, which I was very fond of, to Nekram, one of the bearers, and bade him take care of it. He received it without a word. Some months afterwards, when I was at Cawnpore, and communication with Agra was not yet opened up, I was sitting in a verandah, when a grimy figure in torn clothes, sunburnt and travel-stained, fell, as it were, from the sky at my feet. He took off the greasy coils of his turban, let down the long tail of hair worn by the bearer caste, and from amongst its plaits took out the old family seal! Nekram had not belied his trust: he had struggled through the turbulent country-side from Agra to deliver this seal to its owner.

There was one member of the household not told of our departure, and as he afterwards became rather a notoriety in a small way, I may just mention who he was. The first Bishop of Madras, named Corrie, was a relative of mine. Appointing him to Madras was an instance of putting a round man in a square hole, for he had been one of the early Missionary Chaplains, a contemporary and friend of Martyn, Brown, Thomason, and others, and had spent his whole life in Bengal and the North-West. He was fond of proselytising, and having, like other Evangelicals of that day, rather perplexed ideas of the tenets of the Latin Church, had considered it a triumph of the Gospel to receive into his own communion a young Catholic, whose full names were Joseph Emmanuel De Bourbon. The convert was of astounding parentage, his father being a French half-caste in the military service of Bhopal, and his mother of Armenian, or half-Armenian origin. He spoke English very fairly, or, at any rate, with only picturesque inaccuracies; and, having a certain readiness about him, had been employed by my uncle in preaching, and, indeed, had been taken by him to England, where he had appeared on religious platforms in the capacity of "Our Indian Brother." When I was at Agra he found me out. He was in poverty —living, entirely in the native fashion, in the bazaar. His lodging was in Padretollah, a quarter where priests have been located, more or less, since the days of Akbar. It is right, however, to say that though Joseph retained to the last a great love of the priests, he never showed any wish to return to his old Church. There was a slight trace in his manner to me of the sentiment that he was one of the achievements of my family, and as such fairly chargeable on my civil list. So by degrees he often came to eat at my place, and at last to live at it. He regulated his habits entirely after Indian models, with the exception of sitting in a cane arm-chair, and using a small round table. He was now very old, apparently infirm, and capable, moreover, of passing as a native without difficulty. To take him on a wild and uncertain journey was thought impossible, and there seemed nothing for it but to privately commend him to the good offices of Badul Khan, who promised faithfully to look after him, and to keep him in ignorance of our movements.

The last dinner having been discussed, we drank "To a

lucky excursion," on the roof of the house. Then we descended quietly to the porch. It was past eleven, and a darkish night, and the forms of our horses, and that of a dog-cart, on which our slender baggage and some money-bags were placed, were only dimly discernible. Three sowars, who had promised to attend us, were duly present. To dissemble the gravity of the moment, I said to Badul Khan: "You will be sure to take care of the canary and the little red parrot!" The answer implied a quite solemn acceptance of the trust.[1] Then "Salam Sahiban" was murmured by many voices, and we slowly moved off. When we got out on the country road, under the trees, there was a sense of relief! The doubt and anxiety passed for the time; the step was taken, and we had to make the best of it. I was rather on the look-out for the prisoners from the large jail at Allahabad, for some had been seen about the day before, at Futtehpore, and one of our party had met a man with a cricket-bat, which looked like the proof of some looting expedition. But no, we met no one; and kept quietly on our way, not caring to reach the Jumna before daylight. The fields lay very still around, and there were no sounds but those of night birds or jackals, or a watchman shouting from a distant village. There was, however, a place some little distance from the river, big enough to be designated, in up-country phrase, a "bustee," and this had a bad character. The people were often implicated in boat robberies. It lay off the road, but a single street straggled out, and the traveller advanced for a short

[1] The birds were taken to Allygurh and made over to an old friend of mine, a Rajah in the district. But he, poor man, was himself looted by Mewaties, and my cages passed into that lawless tribe.

way between houses on both sides. The word was passed to trot through this. It was still dark, and there were no lights in any of the little shops. The horses' hoofs sounded on the metalled road. Good heavens! what a hornet's nest we disturbed. We heard afterwards the place was full of convicts. There was a sense of pursuit and the avenger, I suppose, in our rapid passage. From every roof-top there were shouts: men who had been crowded together in sleep sprang to their feet, and cried out as if phantoms were upon them. The change from the silence to this hubbub was very striking.

However, we held on, and soon left the seething village behind, and not long after there came a dim intimation of morning, and we found ourselves in the sand of the Jumna, working our way gradually down to the summer breadth of water.

But there was no bridge of boats; it had been broken up, and the boats taken to the other side. However, we spread ourselves out on the edge of the stream so as to be as conspicuous as we could manage to be, and shouted to the ferrymen. There was no answer for some time; at length a voice said with a good English accent, "Who are you?" We explained, and then the voice replied: "Wait a few minutes, I come at once." A boat came across, and the owner of the voice turned out to be a clever and pleasant Mahomedan gentleman, who was Deputy-Collector at Banda. He little knew what singular adventures were before him, for up to that time his life had been merely one of official routine. In a year or two from that June morning he was a convict in Rangoon; and not only so, but municipal officer of the town, and married to a Burmese lady. He explained to us that for fear of the village we had hurried through, he had taken the boats to the other side. We, of course, made the best of our story, and said that we had withdrawn for a time from Futtehpore, and hoped to re-occupy it soon with troops; which re-occupation indeed took place within a month from that date. The Deputy was friendliness itself—said he was in tents to watch the river, but on account of the heat occupied a serai in the daytime. This building was at the edge of a good-sized village named Chilatara, on the bank. It was a large enclosure, with brick walls and double gates, and lined with rude apartments. Our host begged us to make ourselves as comfortable as we could, and he would swiftly provide something to eat. We all made such a toilet as was possible, and the little bag reminded me, sadly enough, of my two Hindoos the evening before. Then came tea in little red earthen jars, and some curry and chupatties on plates of the same ware. As the heat was stupendous, I had proposed that we should ride on in the night. But about 1 p.m., when most were asleep, the Deputy came to me and said the village was growing rather uproarious. Whether our sowars had suspected we had money in the dog-cart, and had told the villagers so, I cannot say. But there was evidently an intention to create an alarm, in the hope we should go hurriedly off without the dog-cart. Up to this, though one's orders had not been worth much, still some sort of authority adhered to us, and the behaviour of the people had been respectful. But after the Deputy had gone to see what the state of things really was, two Government *peons*, or messengers, came and sat ostentatiously near me. "I say," cried one, "what would you give for this thing?" holding up his chuprass, or brazen badge. "Four annas," his comrade replied. "The brass is worth that—but the Government?" rejoined the first speaker, with a sneer.

The Deputy, on his return, declared that we must start at once for Banda, as the road would not long remain clear. Whether he had really received intelligence to this effect may be doubtful, but we gathered round the dog-cart, and conducted it like the Ark of the Covenant. On getting into the road I looked down the street of the village. There was a considerable crowd of peasants, but most of them were sitting down: some at shops, some on walls, and other elevated places; and there was a tall, stout Zemindar, with a sword in his hand, gesticulating and apparently addressing those present. The Deputy, as he was engaged in ordinary work, including police duties, had with him what is called his "Havilât," or body of persons under trial, and, to take charge of these, a few Nujeebs, with muskets. It was suggested the Havilât people should be let go, and our movements covered by the Nujeebs. This was done. The Nujeebs, who had previously loaded, were drawn across the road, and stood there, till the dog-cart, at any rate, was in safety. The Deputy's tents were being packed; but as soon as the Nujeebs turned towards Banda, the villagers ran in and looted the carts.

However, we moved on. I had been anxious that the sowars should accompany us, not for protection, but to prevent the appearance of our being deserted by our followers. They had not intended going further, but I would not be denied, and they came. The heat was, of course about all that India can do in that direction; but I could not complain, for, personally, I obtained some protection, as I told the syce to lead my horse, and sat with the Deputy in his little buggy. We reached a large village, and stopped for a few minutes to wash the mouths of the horses, and rest them a little. At this spot, of all conceivable places, a European came up and spoke to me. I could scarcely believe my eyes. What was he doing, at such a time, in a remote village of Banda? He said he was an apothecary, and bound for some military station further South. Apparently quite ignorant of public affairs and the state of the country, he seemed to be taking things perfectly easy. However, when matters were explained to him, he went and got his wife, who was in a serai—a Eurasian girl—and he and she stowed themselves away in an "ekka," or little covered car, and prepared to accompany us. As I was sitting with the Deputy, one of the Nujeebs came up, and nodded significantly towards Banda, as much as to say: "You had better move on." The villagers looked furtive and odd, and exchanged glances in a curious, undecided way. They were anxious to know if the Deputy was coming out again, and laughed amongst themselves when he said he was. He took the Nujeeb's hint and proceeded.

The great heat declined, and it was about five o'clock when we saw, ahead of us, horses, men, and a carriage under some trees. The Deputy told me he had sent a messenger early in the morning to the Magistrate, to say we were coming: he did not tell me what I believe he had added, that we thought he ought to come in with us. The group under the trees was waiting for us. There was a large coach, a regular drag, in fact, belonging to the Nuwab, with four good horses to draw it, harnessed for four-in-hand. A coachman drove the wheelers with one set of reins, and an off-hand young Mahomedan, who said he "trained" for his Highness, sat beside to manage the leaders, their reins being quite separate. This strange collaboration worked better than might have been expected. The horses, indeed, were rather full of corn and high spirits, so they occasionally got into confusion, being all jumbled together as if they were playing at football, but the crown of the road was kept, and no accident happened. The two men on the box were civil enough; but two others behind, where I occupied the guard's seat, showed the influence of the hour, and were very sullen. The Deputy stuck to his buggy, and engaged to pilot the apothecary and his wife to a place of safety in the city of Banda. We reached the station when night had fallen, and were taken to the Magistrate's house.

Mr. Mayne, to prevent alarm, and keep things quiet, very properly assumed an ignorance of the crisis fast approaching his district, and expressed great regret that the Deputy had left his post on the river. He gave us an excellent dinner, and provided us each with a portion of a room. But our night-ride, our exposure to the heat, and the reaction from excitement to comparative peace, turned us into pillars of torpor, and though we got through the meal, Mayne had great difficulty in clearing his dining-room. One man got as far as the sofa, on his way to bed, but was hopelessly asleep on it in two minutes. Another fellow, when pressed to retire, rose up, turned round once or twice, sank back and dozed off again in the same chair. But rest did its work, and in the morning we were all right again. Of course, I told Mayne that I considered myself under his orders, and would undertake any task he liked to entrust to me, and the others, I knew, would all help. When, however, the Magistrate was not engaged in keeping up the spirits of other people, I could see that his own were at a very low ebb.

There was a body of Native Infantry of the first Regiment which had given signs of disaffection. The Nuwab was friendly, but at that time without much influence. News of fresh misfortunes kept coming in every form from the different Tuhseelees, or Sub-Collectorates. Either some underling wrote that the Sub-Collector himself had disappeared, or a Sub-Collector wrote that his chest had been robbed, or some busybody sent intelligence that Sub-Collector, chest, and all, had been seized by an aspiring farmer. Certain independent chieftains, however, beyond our border, both continued to send friendly messages and even to supply matchlock-men, so that, for the moment, the station was fairly quiet, and, as yet, in no way untenable.

II

SCENES AT BANDA

THE Magistrate, as has been said, occupied his own bungalow, and the three officers attached to the wing of Native Infantry lived in their usual quarters. It cannot be doubted that our passage through the district aided in bringing the brooding mischief to a crisis. Mayne was displeased with the Deputy-Collector for leaving the riverside; but it is doubtful whether he could have retained his post more than a day or two longer. For, very shortly after, it was reported that a body of Irregular Cavalry had crossed the Jumna at that very place, had raised the green flag in the village, and had had the new proclamation announced by beat of drum:—

Khalk-i-Khuda.
Mulk-i-Padshah.
Hukm-i-Sipah.

That is to say—"The World is God's; the Empire the King's; the Army is in command." We had a right, of course, to expect all Government servants to be staunch and loyal; but, perhaps, allowance was not always made for the fact that many of the subordinate officers were not by nature suited for posts of danger, nor had they ever professed to be able to meet trying emergencies. Mayne was a sanguine man, and, up to the time of the disturbances, had had a firm hold of his district; but he could not conceal from himself that his authority was crumbling away, as bad report succeeded bad report, and the Thanas and Tuhseelees were, one after the other, isolated from the sudder or central station. He placed some reliance on one or two native chiefs; and to a certain extent they did, it is believed, prevent outrage getting the upper hand. At his request some of our Futtehpore party patrolled the city on horseback before bed-time the second night.

The larger merchants had engaged bodies of matchlockmen, who sat before their doors, or occupied balconies, armed and dressed in a manner highly picturesque, if only of partial efficiency. On the third night, however, of our arrival, just when we were thinking of starting citywards, there was a cry of fire, and going into the garden we saw that a bungalow in the lines was burning. One of the officers, Fraser, soon rode up, and with the most praiseworthy desire to prevent anxiety said he thought the fire was a mere accident, and that, in the hot season, thatch and timber did get uncommonly inflammable, there could be no doubt. This, perhaps, was not very satisfactory, but we thought it would do for the city. When we got down there, however, we found a good deal of excitement; but we explained to several groups that an accident had occurred through the extreme dryness of the weather, and as the fire really was put out, and no other bungalow caught, after a time some degree of confidence seemed to be restored.

It was on the third morning, I think, that an astounding spectacle broke upon my view. Who should walk in, important and serious, to be sure, but still in an ordinary sort of way, but Joseph Manuel? It has been said his habits were mostly native, and his dress that curious compromise affected by native Christians, smoking-cap, chupkun and shoes with strings; but on this occasion he appeared in the character of a fukeer—a loin cloth, and another miscellaneous cloth tied round his head. He stated that Badul Khan had been willing to escort him to the West, but that he had dreaded the journey, and had gone into the town to see if anyone would give him shelter. Finding, however, that the Mussulman faction was entirely at the head of affairs, he determined to start at night, and try to join us. It was from him the particulars of poor Tucker's death were obtained, and I have reason to believe they were substantially true. One point only has been omitted from his narrative. He always stated that the Deputy-Collector, Hikmut Oollah, was present, and, indeed, read passages from the Koran. He was probably mistaken in this particular. The Deputy was a timid and wavering man, notwithstanding his abilities; and there seems no doubt, from what came out at his trial, that he was not at first disposed to take a prominent part in the revolt. Of course, Joseph's appearance filled one with remorse for having left him; but his restoration to strength and endurance during these troubled times was altogether a phenomenon—a possibility upon which no one could have reckoned. He had escaped molestation on the road, passing as a mendicant, and, indeed, one Zemindar had ordered him food, and begged him to rest himself. Wonders were not to cease, for, scrambling along at night, and purchasing shelter from poor people by day, a young clerk, the only one that had remained at

Futtehpore, but who, at the last moment, could not be found, and who, as we took it, had made off—turned up in Banda, and could only explain his disappearance by a bout of dissipation, which, at least, seemed strangely unseasonable.

Inquiries plainly showing that the bungalow had been fired by the Sepoys, Mayne very properly thought it necessary to take certain precautions. Some of the small community had, at the Nuwab's invitation, taken up their quarters in his Palace, and Mayne thought it would be well, for a time, at least, to abandon his house, and move also to the Palace, whither the Nuwab was anxious he should at once come. So we all abandoned the bungalow, and went down to the town. You entered under a handsome gateway, and then found a large enclosure, on one side of which was one of those picturesque buildings based on Mahomedan architecture, but not devoid of incongruities and hybrid additions. There was one large hall, sufficiently enclosed, and provided with means of cooling the air, lofty and spacious, full of all kinds of old furniture, crockery, ornaments, and rubbish of different kinds. This was our saloon. Men slept in the verandah around this place, and the two ladies in little inside apartments. The imagery of that Palace was easy enough to take in at the time; but it has not been so easy to get rid of again, and I suppose it will remain in one's mind, as long as life lasts, connected with the ideas of suspense, anxiety, and mental trouble. The nights were fatiguing, for, in addition to the heat and mosquitoes, there was constant disturbance. Chowkeedars came and bawled, sentries kept shouting out, and patrols of sowars frequently rode by. Memory recalls most vividly the ring of the hoofs, the jingle of the bridles, and the excited voices asking for and giving the pass words. The Nuwab was very civil, and we were well provided for. He was a youngish man, small and slight, but very active in frame, and with a lively kind of fatuous manner about him. Very badly brought up, and pampered with every indulgence by his elder female relations, he had gone wrong, morally, pretty well as far as he could; but his natural disposition was easy and good-natured, and he seemed free from resentment, for Mayne had naturally often had to thwart his wishes to keep his property straight at all; but he showed no alteration of manner in face of the misfortunes which were threatening the British power. Once or twice he came in the evening and sat with us, and I remember his offering a small contribution to the general entertainment. He had a figure, a leopard or something of that sort, whose head was secured by a magnet, and could be separated momentarily from its body. "His Highness," cried one of his household, "will now cut off the head of this little animal." His Highness was scarcely equal to the task, having had rather too much liqueur, aniseed, or what not, and was, moreover, seized with a fit of hiccups. With the assistance of an attendant, however, he at last succeeded in decapitating his leopard, and general applause succeeded. Like most native households, the Nuwab's establishment contained one or two Christians of mixed parentage, who filled different posts connected with the servants or the estates. There was a handsome young man named Bruce, who was Agent in village management, and a stout, dark man called Captain Shepherd, who was supposed to command a heterogeneous lot termed the Palace Guards.

Matters were growing worse daily between the officers

and the Sepoys: the former, indeed, went as usual to the lines, but they prudently abstained from giving direct orders, as insubordination was clearly abroad. Mayne had got an idea into his head that an old dismantled fort on the river Cane could be made sufficiently defensible for a refuge in case of an outbreak. And he had been making some preparations for supplying it with guns and having tent equipage taken down there. The idea of retaining his station did him honour, but this particular scheme was scarcely a practicable one.

Be that as it may, in the course of his arrangements he thought that two old guns, which were located at his jail, had better be removed to the fort, both to be out of the way of the Sepoys and also to be safe in his own possession. But when he sent carts and men to the Darogha for the removal of the guns, this ominous answer was returned: "The Subahdar Sahib says 'No.'" There was no mistaking that, at any rate. The Subahdar had come to visit the guard, had observed the carts, had asked their object, and knowing it, had said "*Hookum nahin.*" This news came early in the morning, I think, and naturally agitated Mayne very much; who felt that there was scarcely room in so small a place for two Kings of Brentford. So he went to the Nuwab, and asked if he would assist in compelling the Sepoys to give up the guns. The Nuwab replied that he certainly would, and the morning was spent in arranging plans. The Sepoys had altogether broken with their officers, and these latter had come over to the Palace. We had dinner between three and four, and Captain Shepherd was got up in uniform, and highly important; but it was observed with some dismay that he was taking a very great quantity of sherry. The evening came slowly on. The Nuwab had perhaps some twenty-five sowars, got up in the theatrical tag-rag style of Palace troops, and some fifty Sepoys. Arrangements had been made about our different duties. Mayne and his compeer Webster, a fine, well-mounted man, quite in his element in an emergency, and one or two others were to accompany the party, and, Captain Shepherd having fallen asleep, Bennett, one of the officers, was to command the Sepoys. Others were to look after those left in the Palace. The Cavalry was to be under the Nuwab himself. He got himself up in a red chupkun, wore a sword on each side, and was greatly amused at his position. "This is strange! Fancy me in battle! Of course I have often knocked over things in the jungle, for sport, but I never killed a cat in anger, and now imagine!—killing a man!" I believe he was quite sincere, and had no idea of what was going to happen.

The muskets were piled in the courtyard, and everything was prepared for the expedition. The plan was to march to the jail and bring away the guns. If the Sepoys offered no resistance, well and good; if they did, an attempt was to be made to take the guns by force. The Nuwab got on his horse, and put himself at the head of the sowars, who were all drawn up in a line by the gate. Mayne said: "We are all ready now"; and Bennett, who was a very tall man, stepped forward and gave the order: "Unpile arms." Not a man stirred! Bennett turned to the Sepoy next him, and saying: "Do you hear the command?" pushed him forward. An old Jemadar of the guard immediately drew his sword. "What!" he cried, "is a Sepoy to be struck like a coolie?" Then complete confusion reigned for a few minutes. The men all rushed to their arms, amidst loud cries of "*Deen! Deen!*" (the Faith!) and ran tumultuously out of the gateway. The sowars hesitated for a moment; but one of them setting the example of decamping, they all galloped out of the enclosure, leaving the Nuwab on horseback—by himself! He dismounted and came up to Mayne. There was no appearance of duplicity about him; he spoke quite collectedly and to good purpose. "This is no place for you any longer," he said. "When my own servants disobey me I am powerless. I recommend you to go to Nagode. Stay here, if you like, to-night. The Palace is at your disposal; but I say again, I cannot trust my people any longer." I think it due to the memory of the Nuwab, who afterwards pleaded the excuse, to declare that my impression is that Mayne *did* say: "If I do go, I delegate my authority to you, and you must hold Banda for the British Government."

Attendants were clamorous for the Nuwab to go within the private apartments. They closed around him and carried him off. Other influential natives came up and strongly urged Mayne to go before the guards returned. The decision was taken. There was some little hurry and scuffle. A phaeton, a dog-cart, and a buggy were got ready. Someone touched my arm, saying: "Here is your horse." I mounted my grey. Guided by instinct, but under no special orders, we formed a cavalcade. Joseph was promised a lift, together with some office hands, in a miscellaneous conveyance. The ladies came out and got into the phaeton. Mayne had some sowars with him; but my three Futtehpore men did not show themselves. The sun had gone down just as we passed out of the gateway.

III

NOMAD LIFE

Our departure from Banda came very suddenly at last, but Mayne, though his mind dwelt on his proposed refuge on the river Cane, could not but be aware that chance would likely enough decide our movements, and had felt anxious about Kirwee. For at this outpost Mr. H. E. Cockerell was endeavouring to keep authority. Mayne had written urgently to him to beg him to come into the station, and we had been expecting him all day. The necessity for our abrupt abandonment of the Palace was that it was obvious the Nuwab had for the time lost all authority. Had his men returned with the Sepoys there is no saying what might not have happened. One or two clerks and others in connection with Mayne's office kept their eyes on his movements, and were quite ready to start with us; but those employed by the Nuwab had confidence in him, and preferred to remain.

We got clear of the town without opposition, and, indeed, without notice, and were passing under some trees in the now fading light, when a crash was heard ahead, and, riding up, I found that the Judge, who was driving a one-horse phaeton, had missed the road, and upset the vehicle into a ditch. There were two ladies in it, and one of them, Mrs. Webster, was obviously hurt, though she made very light of it at the time. The carriage was wrecked, and had to be left, and its occupants distributed in the available traps.

Some sowars who had accompanied Mayne—indeed, two were mounted on his horses—took advantage of the imbroglio and galloped off. But two others who were in front, and could not well pass us, shared our fortunes. This is merely mentioned as one instance of many, in which natives seemed to act in the matter of fidelity on the mere impulse of the moment. As we got into the open, the sky behind us began to redden, and then, from the spreading glow, shafts of fire shot up into the air, and the illumination extended to the zenith. The Sepoys had made a bonfire of all the bungalows and public offices. The effect was most striking as we slowly pursued our way along the road, rendered doubtful and gloomy by the sky at our back. Far into the night the fire blazed and quivered above its own smoke, and it was almost morning before the last lurid streaks died out of the horizon. The word was passed down about midnight to be cautious, as a turbulent village had to be passed. But sleep had calmed all passions, and as we moved through the irregular street, there were only the watchmen with their bamboo staves, curious to know who we were, but too excited and frightened to ask. As the first light of the day broke, we reached another small place, where there was a pond, and here we halted for a few minutes, and rode into the water to cool the dusty legs of the horses. Uncertain as the future was, it was an immense relief to be free—to be out in the open air—and no longer subject to apprehensions and anxiety. Scenes in "Gil Blas" and other picturesque fictions occurred to the mind, where the hero had been in a terrible fix—lodged in prison, or bound by robbers, and by some sudden turn of fortune found himself his own master again, on the highway, prepared for new characters and fresh adventures. One's spirits rose, and what was coming seemed of little importance in the delight of having got rid of the odious past.

The Sepoys at Banda belonged to the 1st Regiment of Native Infantry, a party of them had been sent with treasure to Nagode, and it was now time they should be back again. But, although they were almost momently expected, little uneasiness was felt, as all our party were armed, and there seemed no reason to suppose the Sepoys would provoke a quarrel in which there was nothing to gain. Still it was just a sensation that it would be pleasanter when the meeting was over. After leaving the village we came to a ridge, from which there was a long slope leading down to far away, and ending in a stream. As we were descending this—the declivity was very gradual—we saw dust at a great distance, and this developed into a body of men with carts approaching. It was undoubtedly the treasure party. We closed in a little, and awaited events. Sepoys by themselves, on a warm day, get rid of their pantaloons, and array themselves in their comfortable loin cloths. Then they put handkerchiefs under their shakos; but, somewhat ungirt as they looked, they all had their muskets over their shoulders, and advanced, keeping abreast of the leisurely bullock carts. There were three of the officers of the 1st with us, and Bennett, by his height, was distinguishable from afar. We passed each other quite close.

The Jemadar saluted Bennett, and, as if explaining his

position, said: "We are returning to Banda, Sahib: and you?" Bennett answered he was going to Nagode. "Shall you be back soon?" the other asked, as coolly as could be. Bennett replied that his movements were uncertain. The Jemadar then saluted again, and went on. A more singular interview, surely, has not often taken place.

There is no wish to add to the numberless pages in which the Mutiny has been discussed, but every eye-witness is bound to testify how far the occurrences struck him as a Revolt, because this certainly affects the serious question of how the country was governed. People do not revolt if they are happy. Now, in Futtehpore, what had been witnessed was a claim on the part of the Mahomedans to resume an authority which they considered the English no longer able to wield, the cause of this impotence, be it remembered, being the disloyalty of the Native Army. Then, besides this, there were the high jinks of a peasantry, poor and ignorant, intent on loot, and dissatisfied with Government, not because it was the English Government, but because it was Government. And this is the Nemesis of despotism, that the people are bred up to look on Government as boys look on a school-master. To be obeyed, if you must; and hood-winked and cajoled, if you can. Here, then, on this long slope, where we met the Sepoys, we saw a wonderful sight. The peasantry swarming into empty bungalows at Futtehpore looked like revolt; but here we saw them literally scampering over the country like so many monkeys, doing mischief in each other's villages, and occasionally having a turn up with lattees or quarter-staves in the open. This was clearly Outbreak, not Revolt. Whether the peasantry were poor in consequence of the heavy assessment of Banda is another question. All that we then witnessed was the Witches' Sabbath of untaught, needy, unprincipled village roughs—not a political demonstration at all—and I believe the case was at bottom the same in Futtehpore.

It was nearly noon when we reached Kalinjur, and put up at the thana, which was in the centre of the village. We had two doctors with us, one from Futtehpore, and Dr. Clark of Banda, and the first opportunity now occurred of ascertaining how far Mrs. Webster had been injured by the upset. It was found her collar-bone was broken. It is truly wonderful how ladies will endure in silence, sustained by their courage and unselfishness. It was horrible to think what a long night of pain Mrs. Webster must have passed. But she made no complaint. In the village the sweetmeat-sellers were unwilling to serve us, even when money was offered, so that we had to put the coin down and take a reasonable quantity ourselves. In the afternoon, too, a curious demonstration took place. Some Muhajuns, or native merchants, money-lenders, and so on, who had apparently hired men to watch and guard their houses, made them all parade in a procession past our thana. They did not say anything, so the idea evidently was to upbraid us with our loss of authority. There was a disposition, too, in some of the young men towards evening to hang about and interfere with the preparations for starting. However, before sunset we were on the march again, and ascending towards hills which lay at some distance. And as we wound along we kept on our left the wonderful fort of Kalinjur, all dismantled, but still displaying the matchless skill with which an immensely strong natural position had been seized on, and rendered, for all old-world modes of attack, impregnable. Whilst passing this fort, a rifle fell out of the dog-cart, and, going off, a ball was lodged in the fetlock of a horse belonging to Hutchinson, the Futtehpore doctor.

He attempted to extract the ball, but finding it embedded, and supposing the horse would suffer exceedingly from movement, he took off the saddle and bridle, and abandoned the animal by the wayside. But Joseph Manuel, who was seated in some strange vehicle, with clerks and one or two old women, thought the occasion not one to be thrown away. There had been no time at Banda to attend to his wardrobe, and, therefore, he was simply dressed in a loin cloth, and a little linen cap; the heat, indeed, rendered such an airy costume by no means inappropriate. From someone, too, he had obtained a sword without a scabbard, and borrowing a watering-bridle from one of the syces, he secured Hutchinson's horse and mounted him. The animal was quite able to move, and seemed pleased to rejoin the cavalcade, but old Joseph was a most comical sight. Naked himself, on a naked horse, and with his drawn sword held to his shoulder with an air worthy of Marshal Schomberg, he did much to lighten the journey with laughter. All that night the road lay amongst the hills, and surrounded by scenery unfamiliar to those who dwelt in the Doab, but pretty enough as far as the imperfect light disclosed it. The region was part of the territories of the Raja of Punna, and his people were fairly civil. Water was very scarce, and at one or two guard-posts where it was found, they said it was brought from a long distance. The party were willing to pay for it, and the Punna men to accept the offer. Mayne had managed to write from Kalinjur to Major Ellis, Political Agent at Nagode, and that gentleman had sent out a barouche for the ladies, one stage from his station. The ladies got in, and Mayne and I were asked to accompany them.

A few words about Banda. The next morning after the party left was a sorrowful and sanguinary one enough. There is no reason to think that the Nuwab was in any way consenting to the proceedings, and indeed it would appear he was so far a prisoner in his own zenana that his relatives and retainers did what they could to keep him there. The Sepoys and Palace guards, and the rabble of the town, made common cause, and riot and bloodshed prevailed. Those we had passed the afternoon with were all murdered, with their belongings. Poor Shepherd and Bruce, the females of their household, and some Christians in the bazaar, met their deaths early in the morning. Cockerell yielded at last to the solicitations that he should leave Kirwee. But too late. We had hoped against hope that he might catch us up at Kalinjur. But he rode into Banda the day after we had left, before the sun had got hot. He reached the Palace gate, supposing he should soon be amongst friends. But having entered this portal, he was attacked and killed at once. It is well known that the Nuwab received and protected several British fugitives when he recovered authority, and that his mother behaved kindly to ladies. He did very well as long as he kept Sepoys out of the station, and if fortune had favoured him he might have lived to receive thanks and honour from the Government he had seemed anxious to support. But luck was against him. There was, in the end, a great gathering of rebels at Banda, and when they went out against General Whitlock they compelled or induced the Nuwab to go with them. I do not know whether the two swords were in requisition again; but he was taken in arms, was deprived of his estates, put on a pension, and sent to Indore. Thence he wrote to me,[1] being probably afraid of Mayne, and reminding me of the sojourn in the Palace, asked me to exert myself in his behalf. I replied that I had a warm sense of his kindness under trying circumstances, but that it would be mere presumption in me to come forward in a political case. And I could not but add that a home and a pension represented treatment so different from what other nobles in actual rebellion against the British power had received, that it seemed clear his hospitality and friendliness had been already taken into consideration. He died not long after. But a few years afterwards his son actually took a long journey to call upon me, and said he had often heard my name from his father. So the unfortunate Nuwab harboured no resentment. Not being a hero, he did not exhibit heroic conduct; but I believe, if he had been left to follow his own wishes, he would not have rebelled. Worse men had better fortune.

To return to the fugitives, who got into the carriage. We were weary enough, and the easy rolling of the vehicle was very pleasant, and so, chatting away, we found ourselves in the street of Nagode. Looking out from under the hood, I was greatly surprised to see people running about in an excited way, some with bundles under their arms, some dragging children along, all in anxiety and

[1] *See* Appendix No. VI.

expectation. It seemed a straggling, stony kind of place, the shops only occurring here and there; but some of these were closed, and at others the owners were busy fastening up the bamboo hurdles that did service for shutters. We were driving slowly, and at last came to a stand-still, when a tall, middle-aged man, in a sola topee, without a coat, but actively girdled up, and with a sword in his hand, came to the side of the carriage. "You are some of the party from Banda?" he asked. "Yes, this is Mayne, and these are the ladies." "Major Ellis will put up some, and I others. I am Cole, Assistant Agent." "I will stay with you," I said, to make a commencement of the division, and I got out. "Come along," cried Cole; "we will go to my house presently. There is a panic going on, and I like to be here in case of being wanted. I am with the Raja." We went together to some large gates in a native house of considerable extent, and after being subjected to certain watchwords, supplied, of course, by my companion, were cautiously admitted into an archway, and the gates were shut again.

Drawn down exactly in front of the entrance was a six-pounder cannon, or one, at any rate, that looked of that calibre, and in charge, with lighted port-fires, were servants of the Raja, got up in the odd toggery affected by princely retinues in the East. Cole introduced me to the Raja, a thin, rather forlorn personage, who had selected this stormy period for having a sore nose. That organ, naturally of unusual proportions, and now swollen by internal fires, was out of all proportion to the long, thin, Don Quixote face. His Highness kindly took me into a small darkened apartment, where a thermantidote was spinning softly round, and supplied, most thoughtfully, a sherbet of pomegranate or other innocuous fruit, wherewith to refresh the inner man. But there was a sort of ottoman there, covered with cool, white cloth, enticing with soft pillows, and I felt that, come what political changes might, I must sleep. We had been on horseback the whole of two nights, and what with heat and dust, and one thing or another, nature now took the matter into her own hands. I lay down, was asleep in two minutes, and did not awake again till the evening.

The station was garrisoned by the 50th Regiment N. I., and in respect to this corps, Colonel Malleson, in his "History of the Mutiny," writes as follows: "There was one station in Bandalkhand, and only one, in which the native troops stationed did not mutiny. This was the station of Nagode. The regiment there quartered, the 50th Native Infantry, stood firm to the last, fourteen men in the whole regiment having alone shown symptoms of disaffection. Nor was the misconduct of these men displayed until a later period—27th August." From a testimony so honourable to the corps no one naturally would wish to detract by a single careless word. It remains, however, a fact that the news of the approach of the Banda caravan, exaggerated and distorted, doubtless, in native rumour, had greatly excited the men, though the excitement had been admirably guided and controlled by their officers. But the news of a considerable ferment in the lines spread into the town, and though I believe there were no symptoms of outbreak, a regular panic had set in. This was what we had witnessed in the street, and it was against the possible consequences of this that the Raja, with his exaggerated nose, had taken warlike precautions. But when I awoke all was calm again, and the kindly Cole was present to offer the hospitalities of his house. On reaching his bungalow, I found most of the Futtehpore party; and a parcel of rough strangers we were, uncouth in appearance, and retaining little of civilisation except a capacity for good food and beer. We were all most ably catered for by Mrs. Cole, and accommodated, obviously not with bedrooms, but with bedding or wrappings, on which sleep was admirably effected in the verandah. Major Ellis, with whom the ladies and some of our party put up (the rest being received by officers), was a scholar of some distinction, and well acquainted with the history of the part of the country in which his duties lay, the legends of the Bhondelas, Bhagelas, and so on. He had accumulated an extensive and valuable library, and, with the natural affection of a student for his books, felt great apprehension for its safety. He might well do so. During the subsequent troubles of the autumn, the agent only abandoned Nagode for a single night, when he visited the Raja of Punna, who had always asked him to come in case of emergency. On his return, of the volumes and manuscripts he had sedulously collected for thirty years not a vestige remained. The whole library had been reduced to ashes.

Kindly treated and comfortable though we were, Macnaghten and myself were very anxious to push on, and get within hail of our Commissioner. The party that had arrived from Banda in some measure broke up, for the officers of the 1st Regiment who had accompanied us were put nominally under arrest, to enable them to account for their absence from their corps. And as the country around was fairly safe, it was not necessary that onward movement should be pursued in absolute caravan fashion. As Macnaghten and I were inquiring who were bound for Rewah, and ultimately for Mirzapur, it was reported to Major Ellis that we were contemplating a start, and, prompted certainly by some good public motive, he wrote an official letter to me saying that, as he might possibly be able to employ our services, he must forbid our leaving Nagode. We wrote back that our move, far from having as its object escape from duty, was simply dictated by the desire to put ourselves at the disposal of our own Commissioner, and we felt sure Major Ellis did not wish to transfer officers from one part of the country to another, without definite authority for the purpose. He wrote back that he did not so wish, and we started.

Old Joseph was still so ill-supplied with clothes that I did not like to take him on, and Cole kindly offered shelter in his compound, so he was left, with sufficient funds to enable him to follow us, if matters got more settled in the Doab. The rains were fully due, but still held off, fortunately, for heavy wet would have increased our difficulties. We were still a large party,—most of the Futtehpore men, the ladies, Webster, and, for part of the way, Mayne. Night, of course, was chosen for our departure, on account of the heat, and with sincere thanks to our kind hosts off we started. The long hours brought us, before the sun was oppressively high up, to Maihere, a very pretty place, with one or more curious conical hills, which, as in the case of most of the phenomena of nature in India, had been appropriated to devotional purposes, and crowned with venerated shrines.

At this place we got on a once celebrated line of communication, the Deccan Road, now greatly superseded by the railway; and on this at stated intervals were staging bungalows, so that without difficulty we proceeded till we reached Rewah, the capital of the independent kingdom of that name. For the sake of accommodation we did not keep always together, but broke up in twos and threes so as to use the bungalows in turn. When the party I was with reached the staging house at Rewah, we were received by a youngish English officer—looking indeed younger than he really was—well dressed, jaunty and amusing, who gave no sort of impression of being in any responsible position, and did the honours of the bungalow as if the poaching of eggs and the currying of fowls were on the whole as important duties as life presented. But this airy and wholly wonderful person was Lieutenant Willoughby Osborne, a young Political, who was performing the astounding feat of keeping Rewah quiet, entirely by himself. A solitary European without a comrade—a soldier, you may say, without a regiment—was by sheer force of character overawing the authorities of Rewah.

The King had made off to a jungle fortress at that particular juncture; but shortly before we arrived a Durbar had been held, where the Sudder Ameen, who was a Mahomedan, had spoken against the British Government, and on hearing him (or learning about him, he may possibly not have been present), Osborne insisted on the King putting him under arrest, and was so urgent that his wishes were actually carried out, and the Sudder Ameen found himself in prison. To give the impression of being generally aware of what was going on, Osborne moved about a good deal, travelling hither and thither on the mail cart still remaining in these territories. As he was passing a village on one occasion, a Brahmin, who seemed to be a man in authority, took the opportunity of calling him what may be translated as a "blackguard Feringhee," or "Frank." An ill-fated speech! Osborne stopped the cart, descended, seized the Brahmin, tied him behind with the horse's heel-ropes, and started again. After a long run of some miles the breathless one was relieved at an uncomfortable distance from his home, with the recommendation to be more circumspect in his language for the future. I hope our company was some gratification, after such anxious solitude, to this brave and remarkable man. His society was certainly most exhilarating to us, giving us increased trust in our cause, and a desire to aid it to the best of our powers.

The rains still held off. One could not but remember how, in former years, one had watched the sky in the overpowering heat for symptoms of coming disturbance, whilst now as great desire was felt that the dry sunshine might last a little longer. It lasted, but the mornings and the evenings were growing overcast, and at length we approached Mirzapore, Bews having given me a seat in his dog-cart, and as we sat there—strange figures wrapt in native blankets—we could scarcely wonder at the rain which descended in torrents, and danced and glinted from its own puddles on the road. On, on—through the streaming streets and under the dripping trees—till we pulled up at the noble old house then occupied by the Magistrate, but afterwards usually the home of the Judge, till, some years later, during my tenancy, it ceased to be so; for the hungry river gnawed the banks around it, and left it—if more conspicuous—uncomfortable, and only moderately safe. We were welcomed by St. George Tucker, brother of the gentleman I had parted from in the little garden-plot at Futtehpore. And standing by him, as his Assistant, was a young man whose subsequent brilliant career is known to all—Charles (now Sir Charles) Elliott. I would mention a trifling incident as illustrative of the times. After descending that remarkable Steep which separates the tableland of Rewah from the valley of the Ganges, we reached a staging bungalow, where a native Raja, belonging to the Allahabad district, was awaiting our arrival. Eggs in profusion, plenty of milk, all the vegetables in season; hay for our horses, sweetmeats for our men—all were forthcoming. And I "must write a certificate" to say how we had been welcomed; for of the loyalty of a Prince, who catered for English nomads without even being asked to do so, who could doubt? "Perhaps I would especially remark that the Raja who held this testimonial had warmly espoused the British side." Would you learn the cause of our host's solicitude? Neill had reached Benares!

IV

MAKING FOR HEADQUARTERS

It was Sunday, but we had lost note of time, and were only recalled to the fact when St. George Tucker suggested afternoon church. The little fabric used for Divine service was just opposite his gate, and was of the order of architecture which might be called "gimcrack." It looked as if one so disposed might lift it off the ground, put a pastille under it, replace it and allow the fragrant smoke to issue out of the little steeple. However, as Tucker simply remarked, "devotion was pretty well the only stand-by left." So we, in due course, when refreshed and dried, assembled and heard prayers read.

The position of Mirzapore was peculiar; the Sepoys had not mutinied, and there had been no outbreak in the city. It was said that owing to the suggestions of Colonel Pott, who commanded the regiment—the 47th—and through whose admirable arrangements it was kept at least from open sympathy with the rebel cause, many of the Sepoys who had saved money had lent it out at interest. Neither a sudden break-up nor a rising of the rabble suited, therefore, the views of these men. Still, the feeling was very far from being one of security; recent events at Benares had created great excitement, and there was the chance that the Sepoys might break out from apprehension of attack;

whilst in the city the merchants and bankers were timid and cold-hearted, and there had always existed, beside and around these, a strong element of bad characters. The atmosphere, however, at the Magistrate's house was one of hope and calmness.

We had, of course, to keep our onward progress steadily in view, and hearing that a steamer was expected with troops for Allahabad, it seemed a good plan to secure a passage, and let our horses come after us by road. Our party had gradually dwindled; the ladies were moving South; on others Allahabad had no claim; Mayne had gone back Rewah way, to remain near his own district. But we were still five or six, and being informed that the steamer had arrived, and having made arrangements with our servants, we went down to the river bank. The steamer was duly there, and we went on board, and found it full of men of the 64th Queen's. We were just arranging to stow away our traps, when Major Stirling, who commanded the detachment, came up, and though he was perfectly courteous, yet he remonstrated, strongly enough, against our coming on board. He said the crowding was uncomfortable as it was, that the boat had knocked a hole in her bottom, which had only been tinkered up, that she moved very slowly, and any additional weight, however slight, was undesirable. Macnaghten, excellent fellow as he always was, keeping the goal steadily in view, urged that we ought to persevere, notwithstanding the fact that we were clearly unwelcome. But Bews and I thought that if the boat was so slow, the object of our going in it was in a measure removed, and at last it was decided that we should land again, and at once start by road. And this we did, returning to St. George Tucker's house, waiting till sunset, and then mounting and riding down to the ferry.

After crossing the river we proceeded gently along—gently indeed, perforce, for we did not intend to stop for more than baiting till we reached Allahabad. About eleven at night we struck the main road from Benares, and found the dâk bungalow, at that point, occupied by English soldiers. There were tents in the enclosure, and a couple of officers were still sitting in the verandah smoking. They were rather entertained at the idea of a small party of their countrymen riding about in the night, and were desirous of acting as hosts. Escorted by them, we visited the kitchen, their messman kindly supplied us with food and beer, and we sat under the trees and discussed our welcome provender. On inquiry it was thought I was the lightest sleeper, so the rest lay down under a neem-tree for a snooze from which I was to awake them. I fastened my bridle to my arm, and knowing that my horse, being an Arab, would avoid trampling on me, or hurting me, I slept myself; but, of course, under my existing responsibility, the sleep was for little scraps of five or ten minutes only, causing me to start each time to wonder why on earth I should be in bed on the ground, and have a horse tied to me. At last it was two o'clock, and I ruthlessly made the others get up, and off we went. I recollect seeing two men hanging on a tree near this place, and in the dim light they looked ghastly enough; but I believe they had paid a just penalty, being two of the Zemindars who had betrayed and murdered young Moore in their village a few days before. We rode on till daybreak, and then, after a little consultation, decided to hold on as long as we could, make one halt, and so push on to Allahabad by night-fall. The weather was overcast, but not wet, and we persevered till past noon, and then pulled up at a dâk bungalow. Travelling was perfectly safe; troops had passed up the road, and, indeed, the journey was melancholy from desolation rather than exciting from adventure.

In the strips of village streets adjoining the highway the shops were latticed up with bamboo hurdles; other dwellings showed traces of having been fired, and there were very few people in sight anywhere. Some unnecessary violence had, perhaps, been shown by those passing upwards, but, of course, much excitement prevailed. Many wild stories of the treatment of isolated Englishmen by natives were abroad, and Thomas Atkins, naturally enough, found it difficult to draw distinctions, so the very sight of a black man made him rather uproarious. We were soon in the saddle again, and reached the ferry opposite Dara Gunj, at Allahabad, by sunset. The river had risen a great deal from rain up-country, and we had some little trouble with the young fellows managing the boats. They were in a flighty, disobedient mood, and on our threatening one of them he jumped overboard, so that we had to be a little diplomatic.

I had written to our Commissioner, Mr. Chester, from Mirzapore, and he kindly came down to meet me in his buggy. Of course he had much to tell, for I was only partially acquainted with the strange events that had taken place at Allahabad. The whole story is so well known that I will not dwell on it for a moment, but I may mention one circumstance I have never seen in print. Besides the trouble which the Sepoys, rebels, and bad characters of the place had given, some difficulties also had arisen from our own countrymen. Indirectly connected with the railway was one romantic and remarkable young man, the son of an eminent geologist, who could not refrain from eccentric acts. When the town was in its most ticklish state, and the Sepoys only too anxious for any pretext for offence, this youth must needs go and shoot a cow that had strayed into his compound. He seemed quite unaware that he had done anything imprudent, and spoke of the animal rather as a *fera naturæ* which he had discovered in his own domain. After the outbreak had taken place, and as soon as our people began to leave the Fort, this strange man was bitten with a desire to become a pirate. He rigged up a boat, put on board a quantity of loot he found lying about, and cruised up and down the river in his mysterious bark, amusing himself, amongst other employments, with a piano he had picked up in some deserted bungalow. That he would have been heard of generally, for good or evil, seems certain, as he was out of the common run, but death from fever or cholera put an end to his whimsical career.

Chester drove me to the *Red Lion*, the name given to a large house which had formerly been occupied by the Judge, but was now used as a civil barrack, and in which were collected a company of local civilian refugees from Oudh, railway engineers, and others. I was introduced to Dr. Irving, who had charge of the mess, and who was good enough to admit my comrades and myself to the privilege of the Club as long as we stayed. We soon sat down to dinner, and then, of course, we heard the current news. Havelock had arrived, and was only awaiting carriage to proceed to Cawnpore. Renaud, of the Madras Fusiliers, had started with his detachment to prepare the way for the coming brigade. We were all talking without special knowledge, and as people do talk who are not behind the scenes, freely and critically, and it may perhaps be added, foolishly. But the general feeling was one of regret that Neill should have been superseded. He had established a reputation for great decision of character at Benares, and he seemed so especially suited for the work in hand.

Then, too, as some delay was now taking place about transport, for which, probably, General Havelock was in no way responsible, it pleased us uninstructed critics to think that Neill would not have bothered about carts and bearers, and that the hitch was the fault of the new Commander. All our beds stood side-by-side; there were five or six in the verandah where I lay; so one could not complain of loneliness.

After breakfast, the next morning, I and another strolled out. It was quite cloudy and overcast, and coming at length to an open space we found a gallows on which nine men were hanging. The odd thing was there was not a soul in sight. There was a bazaar not far off, but it was deserted, and these nine dead men were absolutely by themselves. The state of affairs, when reprisals began at Allahabad, has been described by others, and I have no wish to judge of actions that were doubtless intended to make short work with the disaffected, and so speedily end the necessity of punishment at all. But something was said about "making examples" by stringing up people for slight offences. The nine coolies by themselves seemed to answer that notion. The native community would not have cared a straw if a thousand coolies had perished. It was, I think, on our return from this rather uncomfortable walk that we saw a well-horsed mail phaeton driven by a veterinary surgeon known for his turns-out. By his side was sitting a tall, broad, and full-fleshed man in Khakee uniform dress, and a turbaned helmet. He descended to see the Magistrate, and make some inquiries on business. Very free-spoken, animated enough in his manner, and defiant rather in gesture, he was a man about whom interest was at once excited. As it was the first time I had seen him, I did not know who he was. But the rumour soon spread that it was Neill who had come. Of course, one looked more minutely at him then, for he was quite the hero of the hour, and certainly for decision, command, dash, and all that is necessary to inspire confidence and insure obedience, he looked every inch his reputation.

Chester told me that afternoon I was to go with General Havelock when he started, but it was not certain whether he would be able to march the next day or not. It had not rained since the day we reached Mirzapore, but each evening clouds were thickly collecting, and we went to bed usually expecting a torrent. But the clouds blew off again. Two days, if not more, passed; and at last one morning positive tidings came that the General would start that afternoon. The camp had been sent on a mile or two out of Allahabad, and on the afternoon of the 7th of July the troops left the Fort of Allahabad. I had made all the little arrangements I could; chiefly with the view to great wet, which we knew was upon us. A sergeant's "paul" had been assigned to me, and Bews, with whom I had left Futtehpore, was to share it. A large curtain over an exaggerated clothes-horse will do for a description of a "paul."

We sent on two horses, and, after luncheon, borrowed a buggy—for it had come on to rain outrageously—and drove to camp. The fields where the camp was set up were a sea of mud, and as evening was coming on we struggled into our tent, where we were very uncomfortable indeed. There was nothing to eat or drink; the earth steamed up, and we sat on our beds, drenched as if in a vapour bath. Insects of all sorts were attracted by our light, and either dashed into the flame, or singed their wings and fell on the table. All the noises of the rains were present: frogs and earth-crickets—with, at intervals, the splashing of showers and bubbling of water-courses. Bews and I were laughing at our plight, when I heard my name called. It was Lynch, an officer I had known in the hills. By rapid travelling he had just managed to catch the advance, and he was accompanied by another officer, named Sheehy. They had got leave to march with the force, but no sort of arrangements could be made for them, and so, portmanteaux in hand, they had come to ask for shelter. Four men in a sergeant's "paul" is close packing; but Bews and I said: "If you can put up with the space, you are welcome to it." They would have slept under a parasol, and were quite satisfied. But the night was wretched. When the bugle sounded at two in the morning the idea of any change was a relief.

V

HAVELOCK'S ADVANCE

THE depression of the night wore off when one was in the saddle again, and as the rain had ceased, and the air was pleasant, by the time the bugle sounded for a halt for "little breakfast," we were all in high spirits. The camp was in a garden of trees, and it was bright and dry, and the soldiers seemed very happy, though they would go out without any covering on their heads, and chose to look on the sunshine as indicative of agreeable haymaking weather in England. I had to assist, of course, as much as possible, in getting up a bazaar for the camp followers, as soon as we reached an encampment; and the difficulty was to prevent the grain and sweetmeat sellers being looted the moment they arrived. However, some help was forthcoming; one or two men had joined as adventurers, thinking there might be posts to fill up if we got settled at Cawnpore. A tall, handsome sowar, who looked very unlikely to be loyal, was attached to my fortunes by Chester, and a very nice young Mussulman, who, by his manners, I should think was of good birth, came to me the first evening in camp, and remained till he met a horrible death a week or two afterwards. Also a capital table-servant volunteered. These little points are mentioned because it never can be remembered sufficiently in the East how the general mind is affected by disaster or success. A defeat—and everyone deserts; a victory—and all throng to congratulate and support.

At first we marched rather slowly, and there was one very sad point about the whole expedition. Sir John Kaye has thus expressed it: "It was a grand movement in advance; but, like many of our grand movements, the heart-breaking words 'too late' were written in characters of darkest night across it." We had, indeed, left General Neill at Allahabad, refusing to believe that Cawnpore was lost. But Havelock knew better. On the 12th of July we started very early—indeed, soon after midnight of the 11th—and presently we came up with Renaud's detachment. The men were drawn up along the side of the road. I remember being struck, in the moonlight, with the yellow colours of the Sikhs. Then we all marched on together, and at last halted a little short of Futtehpore.[1] Barrow had a wonderful Madras servant, who was a good rider, and stayed near him on a spare horse. This man kept a small kettle and teapot slung by him, and sugar and milk in bottles in his *cummerbund*, or waistband, and was game to make tea in no time. He dismounted and made a fire. Willock, of my service, had gone on with Renaud, and, as we had never met, we were making acquaintance. As we were standing together, General Havelock went by—the erect, slight figure, handsome features, grey hair, with the white covered and curtained cap, and the easy seat on the natty Arab—a vignette very familiar to us all afterwards. I think we had got the tea, when bang went a gun, and

[1] Col. Barrow commanded Havelock's handful of Cavalry. He kindly allowed me to join the Mess.

certainly not very far off. There was a complete transformation scene in a moment. Barrow hurried off to the head of his Cavalry, and we saw the Infantry being collected and led straight on ahead, and the guns, eight in number, pushed forward. There were two officers with whom I often found myself—Dr. Domenichetti, in charge of medical stores, and Sibley, an old officer of the 64th, who had grown grey in long regimental service, was, perhaps, of West Indian extraction, and may be called, *par excellence*, "*the* Old Campaigner." He had charge of the Military Treasure Chest. We heard our guns opening, got on our horses, and proceeded along the road. As we went along we came to the dismounted gun at the culvert, and presently to the dead elephant—the results of Maude's two first shots—now historical!

One of our tent companions, Sheehy, was acting as Aide-de-Camp for that morning, and came and told me the General wanted to ask me some questions. So I rode up and told him what the town was like inside, and as he passed into a field near the garden walls skirting the suburbs, I went too, and with me my bearded sowar, Azim Ali.

The General was apparently recognised, for some people behind the walls were plainly taking shots at him. Azim, who was close to me, said, in an undertone:

"*Yih achcha jagah nahin!*" (This is not a suitable place!)

The remembrance of this afterwards made one laugh very much, and in subsequent adventures, when matters occasionally got awkward, the phrase recurred,—"*Yih achcha jagah nahin!*" The enemy made no stand whatever, and really behaved like poltroons; but they were taken by surprise, which perhaps shows that they were not always much helped by the villagers. For they ought to have known exactly where Havelock was. Notwithstanding the barricade, the Sepoys all cleared out of the streets, our troops marched right through, and the camp was set up on the Cawnpore side. I rode through my own little town, and laughed at some pottering improvements which had been thought of, and which seemed such rubbish now. Moreover, they called to mind what I had said to Hikmut Oollah, the Deputy-Collector, that I was going "on a month's leave." I had kept my time very fairly. Here, perhaps, one word about this unfortunate man may be permitted. I see in Kaye's History that, on Joseph's evidence, I accused him of being an active partaker in the murder of poor Mr. Robert Tucker. I was afterwards at his trial, and think it exceedingly unlikely, both from his craven demeanour on that occasion, and from the testimony adduced, that he ever took a prominent part in any active proceedings against the British. He was thoroughly disloyal, and in one of his letters to the Nana, as far as I remember, expressed regret that he should have violated his conscience (*iman*) by serving the English, an odd statement for one of the elect to make to an idolater; but for acts of boldness, daring, or cruelty, he was constitutionally unfit. He died in prison of a collapse of mind and body not long after his case was decided. There was hardly a person in the town. One young fellow, a *jogee* or mendicant devotee by profession, was under the preposterous idea that our soldiers would be interested in his religious freedom from partisanship. I tried to get him away, but he was obstinate, and met his fate, receiving two or three balls into him before he succumbed. Through the town, a little way up the road, I saw some people sitting under trees, and Stuart Beatson, whom I knew, called out to me. So I pulled up, and discovered the General regaling a little, and, being kindly told to join, found a leg of chicken by no means unpalatable. Then came a ride with Colonel Fraser-Tytler to the *Tuhseelee*, or Sub-Collector's office, just to examine the Chamber where the treasure used to be kept. On this journey we saw a good deal of wine and beer being distributed from a merchant's godown, and the General, I fancy, soon ordered it into charge of the Commissariat.

About mid-day, or shortly after, I got back to my tent, and there found some rather unpleasant neighbours. It was understood that Palliser's Irregulars had behaved that morning, when opposed to the 2nd Cavalry, with very lukewarm loyalty; but a small group of them were quite firm, and of these some were killed. Palliser, and Simpson who was with him, were near our tent, and, in honour of the fidelity of those who had fallen, their bodies were laid out in a conspicuous place. Three black-bearded men, olive-coloured in death, with their rigid boots sticking up, were festering in the sun. Sleep came on in the afternoon, and sitting up afterwards, at the door of the tent, I observed a large strong man, with a red beard, lying near, with his head on his arm, and a blue handkerchief with white spots propped on two sticks to make a little shelter for his face.

He was a man of the 78th Highlanders, and some of his mates came presently to look after him. They tried to rouse him, but, alas! he was beyond all appeals. He had been, it appeared, indulging rather freely in the stores which had been found in the town, and, lying down to sleep, had passed away in apoplexy. His name was Campbell. They went and fetched a charpoy, and laid him gently on it, covering his face up in the blue handkerchief he had stretched on the sticks. Then there was something said of another Campbell, and I gathered that he of the red beard had a brother in the same regiment. After a time this man appeared. He, too, had been indulging in more liquor than the weather sanctioned; but he was soon sobered sufficiently to understand the sad calamity. I was forcibly reminded of the grief over the dead fisherman, depicted so powerfully in the "Antiquary." The second Campbell, a younger and slighter man, was distracted with the loss that had befallen him. He sat on the ground, and wrung his hands. "Oh, brother dear!" he cried, "shall I never see you more? Speak to me. Speak to me. Will you never speak to me again? What have you left me all alone for? Brother, brother, come back to me." The bystanders made motions that they would remove the body on the charpoy. Then the younger Campbell threw himself on his brother, clasped him in his arms, and in this way, wrapped in a last embrace, they were both carried away together. I heard the bagpipes soon after, droning in the distance, as the body was taken to the grave.

The station where we had all lived was perhaps a mile off, and I was not able to get up there. But others went, and they found the skeleton of the Judge, which was duly placed within the precincts of the Christian churchyard. The General thought it right that an example should be made of Futtehpore, and the Sikhs were left behind for the not unwelcome task of looting and burning the place. But other work demanded our swift advance, and in the small hours of Tuesday morning the force moved on again. I had, during my brief incumbency of Futtehpore, become acquainted by name with one of the *tuhseeldars*, or Sub-Collectors of revenue. He was a young Brahmin of high family, and had been brought to notice as an officer of exceptional promise, displaying a laudable and apparently natural desire for everything that was progressive and elevated. He had probably less difficulty than others in following his own bent, as his sacerdotal rank screened him generally from coercion. But he seems never for a moment to have hesitated in the matter of loyalty. He made over his treasure chest to an influential Zemindar, and ensconced himself in the same man's mud-fort, till times should look better. When Renaud advanced, he put himself in communication with the force, and, after the evacuation of Futtehpore by the mutineers, sent word to me that he was coming to join us. Unfortunately, though so good a fellow, he did not at all look his character. He was immensely stout, and had a vast crop of hair, with a beard that gave him quite a Saracen's Head appearance. Added to this, he wore a large, untidy turban, which he hitched up in a manner closely simulating rebellion. And before he reached me I am afraid he did not altogether escape rough treatment from the soldiers, who could not understand how a man, whose effigy might have passed in a puppet-show for that of the Nana himself, could be a staunch well-wisher to the British cause. However, when I had got him, I knew his value too well not to try earnestly to soothe any chagrin he may have felt. His unwieldy form and odd, rolling gait soon became familiar in camp, and Thomas

Atkins and he fraternised in a manner which their first meeting gave no grounds for expecting.

The morning we left Futtehpore, as it grew light, people thought more than once that they saw the "twinkling feet" of retreating Sepoys in the hazy distance. And as the day wore on, so strong an impression prevailed, that the enemy's Cavalry were watching our movements under distant trees, as to produce the order for a halt. The objects, though puzzlingly indistinct, were, doubtless, cattle feeding at the edge of groves on the new grass.

Before the halt there had been the tramp of feet, the rattle of the gun-carriages, the creaking of cart wheels, the hum of human voices, and the sudden pause was very striking. For, as the guns were unlimbered, and field-glasses sedulously applied to the distant trees, expectation arrested speech, and there was a dead silence.

At this rather interesting moment there sounded from a neighbouring copse the cry of "*Cuckoo!*" It was Wordsworth's "wandering voice," the companion of the spring-time of our youth, the veritable *cuculus canorus* not often heard, in my experience, so far south in the Provinces of India.[1] Visions of village greens, shady dingles and dells, and the faces of pretty girls were, doubtless, brought into many minds by the familiar note. At any rate, a soldier close to me called out to his mate, in a tone about whose heartiness there was no mistake, and in words whose frankness need not be modified: "I say, Bill, who'd ha' thought o' the likes o' that? Blest—if it was not a damned old cuckoo!"

In the afternoon of the same day it was deemed proper

[1] Jerdon, however, says it travels as far as Central India.

by the General to disarm and dismount the Irregular Cavalry, who were considered to have behaved with more than apathy at Futtehpore. General Havelock superintended the operation himself. It was, doubtless, a most unwelcome duty, and everybody felt sorry for their commander, Palliser. If weakness it is, the weakness is more creditable than some strength—to believe that those who have often gallantly followed you, will follow you to the last. One or two of the native officers, handsome fellows, with that Jewish type of face so common in the extreme North, who looked sorrowful with a haughty, wounded sorrow, refused altogether to avail themselves of the opportunity of going away, and rarely allowed Palliser, or Simpson, out of their sight. Palliser[1] afterwards greatly distinguished himself; but E. H. C. Simpson died in Ireland at the early age of forty-seven. He had a brother who was so embarrassingly like him that mistakes such as overtook the two Dromios were common. It was much easier to manage supplies for the camp bazaar since the Brahmin Deputy-Collector had joined us, and the farmers began to appear. Ploughing, too, for the autumn crops was going on generally, and it was encouraging to think that confidence was being restored. It is quite easy to understand how, after the events that had occurred at Allahabad, the first force under Renaud looked upon their mission partly as an avenging one. There was a slight failure, perhaps, of logic in the idea, because the rebellion was being sternly put down, on the ground that the country was ours; and reprisals, which, against the enemy's property, would have been appropriate, were not so advis-

[1] Sir Charles Palliser died in 1896.

able against the property of our own subjects. The enemy was the Sepoy Army, and, as far as I saw, throughout, though many of the farmers, in whose veins the old lawless blood still flowed, were against order, and in this way, against the British Government, they were not in favour of any other Government.[1]

The "Old Campaigner," when we reached camp, used to come up and say in an undertone something of this kind: "Any sort of vegetables—a little fresh milk—an egg or two, and, of course, if there should be a duck going—so much the better."

The march on the 15th of July brought us to the outskirts of a pretty large village called Aong. The houses were off the road, but there were walled gardens running towards it, at no great distance, and it became evident that there was a considerable force of the enemy at the spot, and that they intended to try and oppose the advance of the column. Here took place what is known as the battle of Aong and the Pandoo Nuddee, fully described by Sir John Kaye. The Pandoo Nuddee was one of those streams which, in the hot weather, present only a thread of flowing water, but are flushed in the rains, their own torrents being augmented by runnels through every ravine. The camp was set up on the Cawnpore side of the river.

And here a strange incident happened. When we were at Futtehpore, just before the outbreak, Bews, himself a railway engineer, was in the habit of hearing from a brother engineer at Cawnpore. The latter was a married man, and it was a curious instance of how our countrymen kept their

[1] Farmers, who had been dispossessed by auction sales, were, of course, against us to a man.

spirits up, that he wrote very amusing accounts of what was going on, which Bews read out to us. It must be remembered that the intervention of the Nana, and his bringing the Sepoys who had actually started for Delhi back again, was a thing which neither Wheeler nor anyone else had ever calculated upon. Therefore, what was apprehended was the first outbreak, and the general impression was, that, if this were got over, all would be well. The last letter Bews received from his friend was to the effect that a row was imminent, but, said he, "we are quite prepared, and if the fellows break out there will be wigs on the green." It was now nearly six weeks since that letter, and though the most ominous reports were current, there was no real certainty as to the details of what had occurred. The spot on the river bank where our little tent was going to be set up was a level area, just below some slightly higher ground, formed accidentally by the action of rains, but suggesting itself as a convenient resting-place, and, as such, it had been apparently used by an outpost of the enemy's Cavalry. For there was some of their rubbish lying there, ropes and straw, and earthen pots, one or two blankets, saddlecloths, etc. Bews had hardly entered this enclosure when his eye caught amongst the litter what he thought was a book. He took it up; it was a leather case. He opened it; it was a miniature of his friend's wife. When I came up I found Bews naturally greatly cut up at the discovery. There was something so very appalling in the mystery of the affair. We never had reason to think the poor lady lived to reach the horrors of the Beebeeghur, and it is not improbable that, in the confusion of moving, the miniature was left at the bungalow, was looted, and accidentally came into the trooper's possession. But that the one man in the force, to whom the fate of the lady was of deep interest, should find this sad memorial of her, was a remarkable coincidence. It would really have been a relief to know that she was dead, and beyond earthly trouble. But the amount of knowledge possessed by the best-informed was only that Cawnpore was no longer holding out. And now, as we all turned in that evening, we felt that we were on the eve of an historical day. Exaggerated accounts of the numbers of the enemy, their force of Cavalry, and the strength of their Artillery, were, of course, abroad, as they always are on such occasions; and it was obviously of the utmost importance to the rebel cause that Cawnpore should not fall into the hands of the British.

We marched at the usual hour, and by the time it was daylight, it became evident that it was going to be fearfully hot. On passing through a village, the Zemindars came out with vegetables and other little offerings, and promised to send supplies on after us for the camp followers. Before noon we reached a small grove through which the road passed, and here a halt was ordered. All the waggons were drawn up, and a kind of zareba[1] was made. In the midst of this a tent was pitched, and here poor Major Renaud was laid on a charpoy with his wounded leg. The fighting men were hastily provided with breakfast and their grog, and after a brief delay, guns and troops moved on. Non-combatants were ordered to remain in the zareba; but my coadjutor, Henry Willock, who was chumming with a doctor, accompanied his friend in the advance.[2] There

[1] This good word is Maude's.

[2] It seems unaccountable that Willock received no decoration.

were a good many of us in our grove—the officer commanding the baggage guard, Commissariat officers, a doctor or two in charge of the sick, a Post Office Agent, and so on. A gun, one of those taken at Aong, was left with us, and was ready to be served by some miscellaneous persons who sufficiently understood the art, and who, in point of fact, did, under excuse of distant objects, fire it once or twice in the afternoon. When the last soldier was out of sight down the road, the curiosity as to the opening of the battle was, of course, great. We had not to wait long. There soon came to us the sound of guns; and, mingled with those of smaller calibre, the deep boom of heavy ordnance. Once we saw some men in the distance, and going a little way out to meet them, found them a small body of five or six soldiers, who had got separated, in some way, from their comrades. They could, however, give no news of how matters were going on. The afternoon wore away, and one good sign was, that the firing, before dying out, was much more distant. Then, as the sun set, we stared at the furthest point of the road we could see, but no figure appeared. Nor, indeed, as far as the eye reached in any direction, did we detect a human being. The "Old Campaigner," who was with us in the grove in charge of his Chest, had, of course, like the rest of us, been on the *qui vive* all the afternoon; but he had reserved a place in his mind for dinner, so that when seven came, and it was dusk, and silence was setting in around us, we were invited to a

He was present at twelve actions with General Havelock; afterwards at the taking of Calpee, and, finally, with General Berkeley in Oudh. A fighting civilian, if ever there was one. He is alive and well, why not decorate him now? The best excuse for mistakes is to correct them.

table under a tree, close by the door of the tent, where poor Renaud was lying. I hope our presence was of some good, for people, in the excitement of moving hither and thither, sometimes made as if they would have passed through the tent, not knowing, doubtless, who was within; and this intrusion we strenuously opposed, for the smallest concussion of the charpoy would have been agony to the patient. After dinner, some little chat on current events, and then to sleep pretty well where we were—not in the last-century sense of falling under the table, but fidgetting into comfortable attitudes on the chair, and at last deserting it for the ground. There were occasional rows in the night, from horses getting loose, and other contingencies; but the morning came at last, and heedless of human conflicts and cares, the birds, finding it was getting light, knew they ought to chirp, and so set to work briskly, though their season of music was ending.

But still no sort of communication from the force, so the Commissariat officers, growing anxious as to how they might be getting on for provisions, determined to start a string of camels. An officer named Thompson being there, and having a horse, agreed with me to move on in search of our friends. We rode a long way, as it seemed to us, without seeing anyone at all. It was an exceptionally hot morning; the rising sun struck us obliquely, and we were much troubled with what the elder Lord Lytton would have called the "glint of the beam." Whilst riding along on the look-out for any traces of conflict, of which the most prominent was a trench dug right across the road, in which big guns had been firmly placed—two of them—as in a battery, I suddenly saw, far in the distance, a great tongue of fire flung up towards the sky, and immediately afterwards, what looked like a vast black balloon ascended, as if in pursuit of it, showing us, in its dispersion, that it was smoke. Then after a perceptible pause there was the noise of a violent explosion, and at the moment I felt a pluck at my knees that made me involuntarily sit tighter. This compression was the passage of the great air-wave, for the Cawnpore Magazine had just been blown up. We were almost beat with the morning sun. I remember I dismounted at a well, and poured water on my head, then got some neem leaves, soaked them, and put them in my sola hat. But even then I was so giddy I could scarcely manage to proceed. However, we approached the cantonments, and found the soldiers all under temporary shelter in the barracks round about, and soon got amongst friends. I saw some men I knew in the verandah of an empty bungalow, and went and talked with them for awhile, and then, passing into a chamber, lay down on the threshold, and in a moment was fast asleep. When I awoke I looked up, and beheld the General entirely by himself, sitting down close by. I scrambled up, and begged pardon for having intruded into the house, which I had no idea had been selected for him. But he was in a most gracious mood, begged me not to go, and said he had read accounts of the war in the Peninsula, and a life of Wellington, by an officer of my name; and then, when I told him it was an uncle of mine, Moyle Sherer, he asked me if he was still alive, and so on. Then he launched a little into the events of the last few days, and spoke with great satisfaction of what had occurred. I remember, especially, he divided the occurrences into grades of importance. "The affair at Futtehpore, the engagement at Aong, and what will be probably known as the battle of Cawnpore." Though exceedingly interested in what he was saying, I took an early opportunity of making my bow, as I was clearly an unbidden though a politely-treated guest. And now, having shaken off the effects of the sun, and got some tea, it began to occur to me that I ought to go into the city. So having found my horse, I went to Colonel Barrow to ask him if he would give me a trooper to take care of me, as I wanted to visit the Kotwalee, the head-quarters of town government, a name still retained under the new police, though the ancient office of Kotwal is abolished nominally, the people insisting on using the word. Barrow consented at once, and as the trooper was Bews, we started, alertly enough, on our mission.

VI

CAWNPORE RE-OCCUPIED

As Bews and I entered the city, we were met by a man with a small kettle-drum; and, without orders, he put himself just before us, and proclaimed the restoration of the former rule. Whether he had in a similar manner proclaimed the Nana cannot well be known; but he diligently rattled away, sonorously shouting an intimation, framed on the same lines as the one mentioned to have been used by the rebels in Banda, but worded as follows:

Khalk-i-Khuda
Mulk-i-Kampani Bahadur
Hukm-i-Sahiban alishan.

We passed through some streets till we reached the principal thoroughfare—the Chouk—at the head of which stood the Kotwalee, a two-storied building, with arches in front, forming a balcony above. Here we dismounted, ascended to the upper story, and were almost immediately surrounded by a crowd of people, many of them Bengalees. They professed themselves delighted with our return; but were rather afraid of the soldiers, and thought that, if measures of retaliation were taken, the innocent might be confounded with the guilty. We said that, as far as we knew, no indiscriminate punishment was at all likely to be inflicted; and told them the best way of showing their loyalty would be to offer their services for useful work. Bengalees are always ready to write; and one of them improvised paper, inkstand, and a table, and commenced writing placards, somewhat as follows:—"This house belongs to one Mokerjea, very loyal subject. Please not to molest." I was requested to sign these, and they were supposed to be talismans, which, when presented to the excellent Thomas Atkins, would assuage that warrior's angry disposition. Fortunately for all parties, Atkins was not permitted to roam into the city; and my talismans were never put to a rude practical test.

Amongst those at the Kotwalee was a tallish Hindoo, of an able but rather forbidding face, who was pointed out by some of the others as the "former Deputy-Collector." I knew nothing about him and had never heard his name before; and, therefore, when he came forward and bowed, and said he hoped our return would be fortunate, I bowed back, and replied that I hoped it would; which, under the circumstances, was a safe, if not striking remark. A rather energetic Baboo, who had been in the Commissariat, having put himself forward, I asked him to remain with me, and help in making arrangements; under his guidance we pursued our way from the Kotwalee, down the Chouk, and out of the town by another way. In course of time we reached Mahomed's Hotel, which had been, as we were told, the headquarters of the Nana; and on stopping, were received by the landlord. I have often thought since, that considering this man had not left his house when the Nana was there, that the building was close to the scene of the massacre, and that English feeling was not in its calmest mood, it showed wonderful presence of mind on his part to pursue his occupation exactly as if nothing had happened. He was quite frank and confident, and from first to last incurred no suspicion, and underwent no troubles. Of course, some months later he had to fly before the Gwalior Contingent for a few days; but he returned immediately afterwards; and I left him, in 1860, hotel-keeping with the utmost composure. Mahomed showed us over the house, and we saw where the Nana had slept, and how another bedroom had been fitted up with *choolees* for the preparation of his food. This word signifies a small structure in wet mud, of nearly horseshoe shape, which, when dry and firm, supports a brass pot over burning sticks.

From the hotel, not a hundred yards' walk led us to the celebrated Beebeeghur. First let me say that this appellation does not mean the "ladies' house," as indicating the spot where the ladies were killed; the building had the name previous to the Mutiny. It was understood to have been a dwelling provided by a European for his Indian mistress, and was therefore constructed in the Oriental style. It was of one storey, with a court in the middle, and a tree grew in the court. Bews and I were certainly among the first who saw it; but Colonel Fraser-Tytler had been there, and one or two others. But there is no question that the aspect of the place, when we entered, was entirely unchanged. It was precisely in the same condition as the first Englishmen who did see it found it to be in. The whole story was so unspeakably horrible that it would be quite wrong in any sort of way to increase the distressing circumstances which really existed. And I may say once for all that the accounts were exaggerated. The attack had evidently been made from the front entrance, and there is reason to suppose that it commenced by muskets being pushed through the venetians, and discharged. There had been a rush across the court to the opposite side, and a mass of human beings were collected in the arched chamber facing the entrance. And thither, doubtless, they were pursued by the assassins with swords. For the whole of the pavement was thickly caked with blood. Surely this is enough, without saying "the clotted gore lay ankle deep," which, besides being most distressing, is absolutely incorrect. Then, as to what was lying about, both of us thought it wonderful that the small litter we saw could be the traces of the numbers who had been shut up there. There is no question in my mind that when the bodies were taken away the place had been tidied a little and painful objects had been removed. There were certainly a few odds and ends of clothing, some locks of hair, some little shoes, straw hats, and so on. Of mutilation, in that house at least, there were no signs, nor at that time was there any writing on the walls. It is well known that there were one or two books, and in them some notes, which have long since been communicated to the public.[1] From this dreadful place we passed down the garden to the narrow well into which many of the bodies of the victims of the assassination were thrown. I say many,

---

[1] A memorandum by a native apothecary was picked up. In this was an entry of a death, thus given:—"A baby,—of itself." By mistake the vernacular word got printed *bibi*, and Kaye (vol. ii. p. 257, Longman's edition) rightly remarks that *bibi* means *lady*. The memorandum or list was in my possession for some time. It was written in the Hindee character, and the word in question took this form, बेबे. English tranaliteration is not possible, but in French *bébé* would correspond. Phonetically, it would be *bay-bay*.

because the receptacle was far too small for all, and there can be little doubt that bodies were dragged across the open space to the river, which was at no great distance. Indeed, we were told as much at the time. When we got to the coping of the well, and looked over, we saw, at no great depth, a ghastly tangle of naked limbs. I heard a low cry of pain, and saw Bews almost crouching with a sickening anguish. There is no object in saying more.

The next day, which was Saturday, the General moved the troops to the north-western point of the cantonment, beyond Nuwab Gunj,[1] and near what had been a Missionary establishment. Conversation had been held about the state of the well, and it seemed very desirable that it should not be left as it was; so, when going over to the new encampment, I thought I would try and see the General on the subject.

The tents had not come up, and I found him sitting on a chair, in a field by himself, with an umbrella over him. I asked him about the well, and said that for one thing, of course, it would soon become very pestilential if something were not done; and he replied: "Please at once procure coolies, and have it filled up with earth." So, getting hold again of Bews, and the Commissariat Baboo whom I nominated as Kotwal for a temporary arrangement, we

[1] I have mentioned in the introduction my visit to the Hillersdons at Nuwab Gunj. When the camp was there I visited the site of their bungalow. Fire had reduced the house to bare walls, and these, again, were stained by the wet weather. I went into what had been a room; the floor was heaped with débris of the fallen roof. Amidst some broken china I found a scrap of paper. On it was printed the single word "Spirituoso." I thought of the music I had heard in the spring.

visited the horrible spot once more, and had the well filled up in a rough manner, and not a moment too soon, for the effluvia was becoming excessively bad. General Neill, on the 25th of July, which was exactly a week afterwards, published an order containing these words: "The well in which are the remains of the poor women and children so brutally murdered by this miscreant, the Nana, will be filled up, and neatly and decently covered over to form their grave; a party of European soldiers will do so this evening, under the superintendence of an officer." But this refers to making the earth thrown into the well level with the surface, and forming a memorial mound to mark the spot. The bodies had, as I say, been covered up a week before; indeed, if this had not been done, the place would have been unapproachable.

Meeting with Willock, I heard of poor Beatson's illness. He had been taken with premonitory symptoms the very day of the battle of Cawnpore; but with indomitable courage he managed to keep with the force, and reached Cawnpore in the evening dreadfully exhausted. Cholera had seized him, and though he pulled through the actual attack he was too enfeebled to rally. I saw him for a few minutes at Suvada Kotee, where a temporary hospital had been established. He was dreadfully altered, but still prepared with his kind smile and an outstretched hand. This must have been Friday evening, and he died, I think, in the night. At the same place (Suvada Kotee), poor Major Renaud had his left leg taken off, high up the thigh; an operation which he only survived one day. Both Beatson and he were buried near the camp at the north-west corner of the station, where their tombs serve not only as memorials of themselves, but as an historical reminiscence of Havelock's position. It was chosen under an idea that an attack might be expected from Bithoor; and though this was a mistake, the distance from the bazaar was favourable for restoring discipline, which had naturally enough been partially relaxed. Stuart Beatson was in the prime of life; and there seems little doubt that, had he lived, his clear head, and high spirit, would have carried him to great distinction.

Willock told me some of the incidents of the day of the battle of Cawnpore. He was close to poor Currie, of the 84th, when he received the terrible wound from a round-shot in the lower part of the body, to which he succumbed. I believe I am able to throw light on one little event of that day, and am glad to do so, because it explains a point which led to some misunderstanding, and it also renders the story, as related by Sir John Kaye, intelligible, which, as it stands at present, some would surely say is not the case. The present Sir Henry Havelock-Allan is mentioned by the historian as having greatly distinguished himself by performing the following action: "The Infantry prepared to advance right upon the death-dealing battery of the enemy, the 64th Foot, led by Major Stirling, in front. At this moment, the General's Aide-de-Camp, 'the boy Harry,' wheeled his horse round to the centre of the leading regiment, and rode straight upon the muzzle of the twenty-four pounder."

It must strike anyone reading this for the first time that what the younger Havelock is related to have done was an altogether astounding thing. Why should he have volunteered to ride in front of a regiment, unless it wanted leading? And what call is there for any one, when a corps is gallantly advancing, to get between it and the enemy's guns? Now for my elucidatory note. People who had got horses were very lucky. They were not easily to be procured. And some of the officers on the march picked up ponies which farmers, or others, were willing to sell. The north provinces' "tat" is an animal of astonishing endurance; but if he be of at all a troublesome disposition, his vices are strongly developed. When of the masculine gender, and untampered with by precautionary operations, he delights in making himself prominent; and he is equally objectionable in his expressions of love and jealousy. Squealing, rearing, kicking, and biting, are amongst his resources; and moments occur when remonstrance and punishment are alike unavailing; and master of the situation, he will neither advance nor retreat, and nothing will please him but pawing the air, lifting his gums off his teeth, and behaving altogether in a manner at once outrageous and unbearable. Now, it so happened that Major Stirling had bought a particularly misguided and undisciplined pony, and the day after we crossed the Pandoo Nuddee, I saw this animal advancing on its hind legs, determined to bite some other horse, if possible. Everybody got out of the way, and I remember the younger Havelock, in joke, drew his sword to defend his own steed. Now, I was told that Stirling was on this beast, that it turned brutally restive, and he, with the intention of sending it at once to the devil, dismounted. There was the briefest space, during which, by a pure accident, the leader was not in front of his regiment. "Come on, then, with me," cried the A.D.C., who happened in that second to ride up. If this incident has been told before, I must beg pardon for repetition; but Sir

John Kaye certainly did not know of it. I believe it to be true, and it is agreeable, because it puts everything right. The 64th needs no eulogy from anybody. Stirling was romantically brave, as his death, a little later, amply showed; while "young Harry" was well worthy of the honours he won, and which he has since increased in other fields of action.[1]

From the position which General Havelock occupied at the north-west corner of the Cawnpore station, he despatched a force to Bithoor. The buildings which had constituted the Nana's palace were, for the most part, destroyed, as well as the residences of his dependents. This is not an inappropriate place to say a word about the Nana Sahib, his habits, and so on. When the massacre became generally known, the Nana grew positively into a European notoriety. The French, with their taste for melodrama, and their perception of the artistic value of contrast, seized on the idea of concocting his personality out of cruel instincts, exceeding those of ordinary barbarism, on the one hand, but with delicate and luxurious habitudes on the other. So that, in their hands, the Nana became a scented sybarite, who read Balzac, played Chopin on the piano, and, lolling on a divan, fanned by exquisite odalisques from Cashmere, had an English child brought in occasionally, on a pike, for him to examine with his *pince-nez.* In England, again, the desire was rather to make out the Nana to have been one of those extraordinary monsters of ferocity and slaughter who were

[1] This anecdote was labelled, soon after its publication, by a military weekly, as "camp gup." But it only professed to be gossip, and is left in as such—*quantum valeat.* Particularly, as Kaye's perplexing account of the incident is retained, intact, in Longmans' Silver Library edition of his history, 1897.

favourite characters in the earliest dramas, in which, as Charles Lamb drolly said, "blood was made as light of as money in a modern sentimental comedy, and as *this* is given away till it reminds us that it is nothing but counters, so *that* is spilt till it affects us no more than its representative, the paint of the property-man."

I remember, when in England, in 1860, seeing a large canvas daub in a show at a fair, which was said to represent the Nana, and he really was a terrific embodiment of matted hair, rolling eyes, and cruel teeth. But the reality was extremely unlike the romance. I have heard from several who knew him, and especially Dr. J. N. Tresidder, who had attended him professionally, that Doondoo Punt was an excessively uninteresting person. Between thirty and forty years of age, of middle height, stolid features and increasing stoutness, he might well have passed for the ordinary shopkeeper of the bazaar, had it not been for the Mahratta contour of his turban, of which, however, he did not effect a very pronounced type. He did not speak English, and his habits, if self-indulgent, had no tinge of poetry about them. He was particular about his *ghee*; loved the eyes of dancing girls rubbed round with lampblack, and their lips rosy with the juice of betel-nut; whilst his ear for music was satisfied with the rude viol and *tom-tom* (or small hand-drum) that accompanied their slowly-revolving petticoats. But of any of the refinements of sensual enjoyment he was wholly ignorant. It was, apparently, a pleasure to him to receive occasional visitors at Bithoor; and he used to come into Cawnpore and give general entertainments, all the arrangements of which he placed in European hands. But his daily life at home was carried on amidst surroundings of expensive discomfort. He was wont to repose on a charpoy (a framework laced with broad strips of cotton cloth, and standing on four legs, whence the name) in a small private apartment, where a loose heifer roamed at will, watched by an attendant, who, in a roughly-wrought silver vessel, caught droppings which, to us, would be disgusting, but to our Hindoo brethren are replete with national, and, indeed, sacred associations. Many months after this July expedition to Bithoor, Lieutenant Malcolm,[1] of the Royal Engineers, with a great deal of trouble, and no small amount of ingenuity, fished out of a large well what was called the Nana's gold plate. This was immensely valuable, because it really was of solid and very pure gold; but it had no artistic importance of the slightest degree. The trays and bowls were of the rudest shapes that were compatible with the purposes for which they were intended, and, in mean material, would not have attracted attention, if discovered in a South Sea Island. The Nana was a heavy, dull man, with a grievance. He thought Lord Dalhousie had treated him very badly by not letting him have the full allowance which was bestowed on the Peishwa, who had adopted him, and this wrong rankled in his mind.[2] Writers who blame Lord Dalhousie for his

[1] Now Colonel Malcolm of the retired list, one of the Malcolms of Poltalloch.

[2] The Nana's claims were unquestionably invalidated by a fallacy. He seemed to think that Bajee Rao's pension was the result of a contract: he to give up his territories, and the Company, in consideration of the fact, to make him a grant. Nothing could be less true. The Peishwa took the field against the forces of the Company, was completely defeated, and had his territories taken from him. Then the Company, in pity for his fallen fortunes, made him a most munificent provision for life.

aversion to recognising adoption always go off into the religious necessity with the Hindoos of having a son to perform the funeral ceremonies, and to attend to the annual commemorations of the dead, and are astonished that he did not take this view of the subject into consideration. It seems much better to recognise adoption; but the argument about the funeral ceremonies is not, perhaps, a sound one. The validity of an adoption, as far as its religious aspect is concerned, does not depend on the recognition of Government. In point of fact, the Nana did perform the funeral rites over Bajee Rao, and kept up the commemoration, though he did not succeed to the pension.

The character of the Nana is so far of importance that it affects the wisdom of Sir Hugh Wheeler, Mr. Hillersdon, and the others who called in his aid, and gave over the powder magazine into his charge. If he had been a far-seeing, ambitious man, of administrative abilities, who was sure in a disturbance to come to the front, the simplicity of those who trusted him can scarcely be called less than culpable. "Almost as soon," writes Mr. Justin M'Carthy, "as the Nana's presence became known in Cawnpore, he was surrounded by the mutineers, who insisted that he must make common cause with them and become one of their leaders. He put himself at their disposal." From everything I have heard, I do not think this is an accurate statement. It is possible, and perhaps probable, that the Nana saw a way to getting his pension by putting the English under a great obligation; and certainly he could not at first come to any agreement with the Sepoys; or at least did not. Critics of Sir Hugh Wheeler's conduct should bear in mind that the revolted Sepoys left Cawnpore, and made two marches towards Delhi. And Wheeler's entrenchment, which seemed so miserable when we came to look at it, particularly when the mud ramparts had been reduced by the rains, proved really enough for what he was guarding against, namely, the confusion incident on an outbreak. But the advisers of the Nana induced him to send messengers after the Sepoys, and offer them ample monetary remuneration if they would return. They did return, and all the world knows with what results. Then the Nana's name became the one to conjure with; but of his individual influence there seems no trace throughout. We know something of what Azimoollah did; and the hand is not difficult to discover, at times, of Jowala Pershad, Baba Bhut, Tantia Topee, and the rest; but the stolid, discontented figure of the Nana himself remains in the background, rejoicing, doubtless, in the success of the treachery, and gladly consenting, probably, to the cruelty; but inanimate, incapable of original ideas, and more elated, perhaps, with the present glory of a hundred guns fired in his honour, than with any distinct idea of future dominion. It remained so to the end; his death even was indistinct and insignificant, shrouded by the malarious Nepaulese forest, and producing little effect but the dispersion of a band of moribund vagabonds.

Henry Willock accompanied the expedition to Bithoor, and brought back two of the Nana's pets, a Wandaroo monkey, and a squirrel quite as big as a small rabbit. The monkey became well-known in camp, and ultimately reached the Zoological Gardens in London, where I afterwards called upon him. The costly squirrel was made over to me; but whether owing to undue excitement, or perhaps change of food—for ignorant of his habits I could only ask, in a helpless way, like the gentleman in "Dombey," whether "something temporary could not be done with the teapot" —he died—poor, beautiful creature.

General Neill (he had just been made Brigadier-General) arrived on Monday, the 20th of July, and as he was to remain when Havelock went on, the local command was made over to him, and he began to try and establish order and discipline in Cawnpore itself. It must be remembered that he had been greatly praised; everywhere it was noised abroad that Neill was the man for the emergency—Neill would not stand any nonsense, and so on. And of course he could not but suppose that whatever position he was in, something marked would be expected of him. Hence some of his orders, particularly the unfortunate one about the cleaning up of the blood; but it remained almost a dead letter, carried out, I think, in two instances. It is, however, preposterous to suppose that men in scenes of great excitement can behave exactly as they would on calm reflection in ordinary circumstances.

Since the publication of Malleson's history, it is now known that Neill carried his exaltation so far as to write a censorious letter to Havelock, when the latter decided to fall back on Cawnpore; to which Havelock replied that nothing but considerations of the public service prevented his ordering Neill into arrest. Impulsiveness was, of course, a facette, so to speak, of that general boldness which made Neill what he was. And he sometimes said things which others would have kept to themselves. He would laugh and declare, not heeding who was present, that "the old gentleman (Havelock) looked upon himself (Neill) as the heir-at-law, so he could not expect to be liked more than heirs-at-law usually are." But this was mere manner: and people are too ready to dwell on these little surface blemishes, not taking the trouble to look for hidden good qualities. I have been told since, that with all his martial bearing and off-hand speech, General Neill devoted much time in private to serious reading, and was interested in questions which we should have thought at the time were more in General Havelock's line.

Two operations were going on simultaneously; every effort was being made for crossing the river, and an entrenchment was being formed on the bank for the garrison that was to be left at Cawnpore. About this time, a resident of Bithoor, a Mahratta, named Narain Rao, wrote to me from there, to say that he had always been on the English side, had been put into confinement during the supremacy of the Nana, and wished to pay his respects to the General. I showed his communication to General Havelock, and he directed a Persian answer to be prepared, stating that he must be quick about it if he did not wish his loyalty to be suspected. The title or sobriquet *Nana* is not uncommon amongst the Mahrattas, and this man Narain Rao was also called the Nana, and it was, in consequence, rather difficult to procure him a civil reception with those who could not make out who he was. He was no relation whatever to Doondoo Punt, but was the son of an adherent of the Peishwa's, called [illegible]e Subahdar Sahib, whom I well remember in Mr. Thomason[illegible] time. He sometimes visited Agra, and was always [illegible] by Mr. Thomason with great respect, as having [illegible]nowledged as a good soldier in his younger days [illegible]n Malcolm and even, I believe, by the Duke of [illegible] The son was very Mahratta-looking. I have mentioned this gentleman's name because some of the stories of the Nana's doings are based upon what he said. But though I make no question of Narain Rao's loyalty, his wish to represent himself a sufferer was so mixed up with the hope of discrediting his brothers, with whom he had a quarrel about a will, that his adventures seem to me apocryphal now that one can think of them quietly. He had entreated me to get a vehicle for him, as he declared himself destitute of all equipments, and a tradesman in the town lent a carriage, but no one would drive it. The young Mahomedan of education and nice manners, who had come with me from Allahabad, was standing by when the dilemma arose. "I will go," he cried, and jumping on the box he whipped up the pair of horses into a brisk trot, and took the road to Bithoor.

We all, naturally, wanted to do something, to show that we were helping the general restoration, and as the city was getting well into our complete control, I consulted the Brahmin Deputy-Collector as to whether we could get men to establish a thana a few miles out of the town. We found people quite willing to take service, and the young Mahomedan seemed the very fellow for the post. Full of go, and anxious to bring himself forward, I asked him if he would try and form a little nucleus of British authority out in the village where it was proposed to place the thana, and he jumped at the idea. He had got a horse of his own, and he started at the head of his little band, who were all armed, and was to engage other men out there if necessity arose. Of course he was told that he was not expected to fight, and if Sepoys approached he was to fall back. But for all purposes of exercising his authority amongst the peasants he was, we thought, strong enough, and he himself was quite confident. He had hardly been there two days when a large body of Sepoys, stealing across from Calpee, and endeavouring to get over the Ganges into Oudh, came suddenly upon his thana in the night. His men made some resistance, but the idea of Sepoys carried a certain terror with it, and the darkness was a temptation to try and escape. The plucky fellow, notwithstanding, held out, and at last fell into his assailants' hands. They bound him, cut his throat, and hung him by his feet on a tree. There are honoured mounds above brave Englishmen all over the world; but that young hero's grave demands a leaf of laurel too. He espoused our cause; he was faithful to it to death; he fell—fighting.

VII

THE RAINS OF 1857

THE wet season had thoroughly set in: the great river was rapid and swollen. And the difficulties General Havelock had to encounter were great; for the boats had to be collected, and boatmen to be procured. This class of men were shy of coming forward, in consequence of the complicity of some members of their craft in the treachery at Suttee Chowra Ghât. The little steamer, however, was of great service, and the crossing was effected in some four days, notwithstanding every obstacle. Colonel Fraser-Tytler was indefatigable. I remember seeing him, one evening, in a little native building by the river side, soaked and daubed in such a manner as rather to resemble a Nubian stoker in the Red Sea than his own thoroughly military and *distingué* self. Of course the troops were moved gradually down towards the Ganges, from the north-western corner of the station, and were passed across the water in turn.

It was before the Force had got fully across, I think, that one morning, when I had returned from riding, I found a middle-sized, strongly-built man, dressed in Khakee (ash-coloured) uniform and a helmet, who had come to look me up, and who asked if I was a civilian who had arrived with the Force. I replied that I was, and he then said: "I am Herbert Bruce, I hope we shall be friends, and work cordially together." He had rather a colourless face, light hair, and very pale blue eyes; but a determined mouth, and altogether an expression of much intelligence. I knew nothing about him, but he told me he belonged to the Bombay Army, and that he had come up to be with Neill, who was very anxious to establish a military police, which would not only act as ordinary city constables, but could be used, on an emergency, for any outpost duty required. From that morning, for some months, I was with Bruce every day, and sometimes more than once in the day.

I waited upon General Neill in due course, and he told me, very civilly, that he had communicated to the Government his wish to have charge of the city himself, and, as it was so immediately near his entrenchment, he wanted the town people to understand that its occupation was, for the present, a military one. He kindly wrote me a letter later on, which I possess,[1] to the effect that the plan was not in any way suggested by the inadequacy of such arrangements as had been made, but merely from his own views of military necessity.

It may as well be said here that the extraordinary rumours that Mr. Grant (afterwards Sir John)—who was directed at this time to assume civil power, as far as it could be assumed, in the districts East of Cawnpore—desired to thwart Neill's plans, were quite certainly without foundation of any sort. Our instructions were to co-operate in every possible way with the military; and no one was so foolish as to suppose it mattered *who* did any particular work, so long as it *was* done! Dear Heaven! it was not a time to bicker amongst ourselves.

[1] See Appendix II.

We had got hold of a great number of papers from the office of Baba Bhut, who was the member of the Nana's entourage to whose administration the district of Cawnpore had been intrusted. It was entertaining to read his orders; some of them exactly the sort of directions one had given one's self when in some doubt what to do next. In the margin of a report on some village disturbance, he would have written: "Make strict inquiries and report again in three days." Deliciously make-believe energetic! These papers, however, gave us a clear idea of who had deserted us and joined the Nana amongst our old officials. One of the most prominent of those who had cast in his lot with the so-called Peishwa was the Deputy-Collector who had received Bews and myself politely at the Kotwalee, and as he had no sort of excuse to make for himself he was condemned.

The site having been chosen by Fraser-Tytler for an entrenchment on the bank of the Ganges, the work was pushed forward as fast as circumstances would permit, and by the time the troops had crossed, the place was in some measure defensible. I got a more comfortable tent, and had it pitched on the glacis, near one of the entrances of the fort. Hard by, some dismantled houses were occupied as outposts.

We seemed a small body, indeed, when Havelock was gone. At first he stayed four days at Mungulwar, a village about three or four miles on the Lucknow road, and naturally some communications were held with the camp during that time. But the force moved away, and though we heard the firing at Onao, no distinct news of what was going on reached us. There were one or two houses more or less in repair within close proximity to the entrenchment, and these were occupied, at least during the daytime, by those remaining with the garrison who had duties to perform. News reached us that the rebels were gathering again at Bithoor, and Neill armed the steamer and sent it thither to destroy the boats, and thus prevent the crossing over of troops. But parties of Cavalry were said to come by night even into the suburbs of Cawnpore; and certainly more than once I heard the clatter of hoofs as of a body of horse on the road. The nights were disturbed, for from the villages, both on our side and in Oudh, there was constant matchlock firing.[1] It was perhaps intended more to frighten intending marauders than anything else; but it produced a general effect of disquiet. The very stout Brahmin who had been a Tuhsildar with me in Futtehpore, and had taken our side so warmly, Umurnath[2] by name, had shown plenty of courage in joining us on the march, and took up his quarters close to mine, making himself useful in every way. But the idea of Cavalry roaming about by night disturbed him a good deal. There was so much of him—such vast protuberances both preceded and succeeded what may be called the original kernel of the man—that a dread of sabres set in with him, and he provided himself with two of what he termed *pahlawans*, or "champions" as the dictionary is pleased to call them. I believe such

[1] One night, when the matchlocks were unusually still, Bruce and I distinctly heard firing at Lucknow. So that I chanced to be an ear witness of attacks both on Wheeler's entrenchment and the Bailey guard.

[2] By an unaccountable slip, called in the "Memories," Kasinath, which was his brother's name. Umurnath was, however, generally known as the Pundit.

persons are got from Rajpootana by shroffs and bankers, and perhaps Umurnath had procured these two from monetary friends in Cawnpore. They were most extraordinary creatures—huge frames with exaggerated muscles, broad tawny faces, surmounted with long hair hanging in thick strips, necklaces of large wooden beads, ferocious moustaches, steel caps under red turbans, voluminous waistbands in which were thrust two horse pistols, a leather strap holding a sword, and a long matchlock carried in the hand. Intending one evening to dine with Bruce, who had his meals in one of the empty houses, I got a tradesman to lend me a mule carriage. I was just getting in when Umurnath came up and asked where I was going. When he learned, he said it would be dark when I returned, and he could not let me go without the *pahlawans*. So he went and fetched them. First, one of these alarming warriors got into the carriage, and established himself in a corner, then I took my seat, and the other warrior sat, with the carriage door open, on the floor. Their hirsute legs, with knotted fibres (or it may have been varicose veins), were wonderful to behold, and emerged from loin cloths with a worked border, terminating in red shoes very much turned up at the toes. I was of course received with shouts of laughter; but my grotesque friends considered me in their charge, sat solemnly in the verandah during dinner, and afterwards escorted me back to my tent.

I had lost my companions: Bews had gone on with Barrow's Cavalry; Willock had got himself attached to the advancing column, and the two Queen's officers had departed too, having had work assigned them. We still heard firing on the Lucknow road; it had got very distant at one time; but on the 31st of July we were surprised by some horsemen riding in, and found that General Havelock was again at Mungulwar. Many sick men came in, and amongst them poor Bews, who had fallen ill with dysentery. He came back to my tent, and rested for a day or two, till, as he was worse instead of better, he took an opportunity of getting to Allahabad, and so our adventures together ended, for he was not able to appear again on the scene. Marriage cards, received long afterwards from New Zealand, were the only token of his existence I could afterwards obtain.

Havelock held on at Mungulwar, and some Infantry and guns arriving from Allahabad, Neill pushed them at once across the river, and thus reinforced, the relieving column again advanced towards Lucknow. Neill was dreadfully disappointed at the first putting back, and, as his manner was, did not hesitate to denounce the movement in energetic terms. There is no question that, elevated as he then was by the general opinion of him, he would have gone on had he been in command; and, however imprudent it might have been, perhaps he might have succeeded. One of those transformation scenes so common in Asiatic politics might have taken place. Nowhere is success so successful as in the East. But still, judging by what did happen when Outram went, perhaps if Neill had got into Lucknow he would not have been able to get out.

Days passed, and we heard distant firing, and firing more near, and it was all very puzzling to make out; when at length the mysteries were explained, and back came the whole Force, taking up quarters in the barracks on the eastern side of the town. Prospects were getting rather gloomy, the ominous word Calpee began to be mentioned for the first time, a word afterwards to cause constant anxiety and trouble. What was called the Gwalior Contingent was a thoroughly efficient body of troops, particularly strong in Artillery, which nominally belonged to Scindia, but had been organised and trained by the British. The rumour was that this small army had shaken itself free of control, and intended to march on Cawnpore, crossing the Jumna at Calpee. Why they did not come is not known. The fact that they shilly-shallied all the autumn, and at last only crossed the river to break themselves to pieces against Colin Campbell, is one of those singular events in which, if the devout think they see the hand of Providence, they may well be excused their belief. Bithoor, too, had become a perfect nest of rebels; and Havelock was no sooner across the river than he made an expedition there, in which there was some stiff fighting.[1] After this there

[1] "Bithoor was defended by several regiments of mutinous Sepoys, including Cavalry and Artillery. They had thrown up entrenchments with some skill, and, besides fighting with halters round their necks, the Nana was defending what was left of his household gods and altars. Havelock's march to Bithoor occupied eight hours, under a Bengal sun, at the end of which time the engagement was severe. The Madras Fusiliers and 78th Highlanders, with my battery (I was ill in Cawnpore), formed the right wing; while the left wing was composed of the 64th, 84th, and Sikhs, with Olpherts's Battery. The force advanced in 'direct echelon from the right' (Havelock's favourite movement). As the Fusiliers moved in extended order on the right, they were suddenly assailed by a sharp fire from a high outwork that had been thrown up in front of a village. Major Stephenson, then in command of the 'Blue Caps,' Neill having remained in Cawnpore, at once wheeled three of his companies to the right, and came to close quarters with the 42nd B.N.I., who really fought with great resolution from behind their 'moorcha.' Havelock said that 'he had not seen fire kept up so well since the days of Ferozshuhur' (in the Punjab). Our Artillery

was a little respite; the Calpee rumour remained a rumour, and there seemed no immediate work to be done. The promised reinforcements had to be waited for. All appeared calm, but there was one heart that was suffering, in noble silence, a great disappointment. Havelock was to be superseded. There was probably not the slightest intention of

meantime carried on their usual duel with the enemy's, but had unusual difficulty in silencing the latter, owing to the protection afforded by the earthworks; so that the rebels had to be driven out of their works mainly at the point of the bayonet; and the principal credit of this hardly-won success was certainly due to the Infantry. The troops bivouacked that night at Bithoor; and, after razing most of the buildings to the ground, returned the next day, in a deluge of rain, to our camp on the Cavalry Parade at Cawnpore. Here is a characteristic story about Anjoor Tewaree, which occurred during the above action. Our famous spy was constantly bringing us the minutest description of the enemy's movements, and especially of those of the Nana and his following. Indeed, the attack was mainly undertaken on his information. But our excellent Q.M.G., who, although a Scotchman, has a pleasant wit, had often rallied Anjoor Tewaree as to his sources of information, asking him where he picked them up, and pretended to disbelieve that he had obtained anything from ocular observation. 'All right,' said the spy, 'one day I'll prove it to you.' As the column were in the heat of the attack of Bithoor, and Fraser-Tytler, as usual in the front, was calmly observing the position and movements of the enemy, he felt a tug at his foot, and Anjoor whispered to him: 'Do you see that bit of white kupra on a tree in front of you? Well, take it down quickly, and put it into your pocket!' Almost mechanically Tytler reached up to the branch, pulled down what seemed to be a piece of cotton cloth, and pocketed it. After the enemy had been driven out, and the action was over, Tewaree came up again, and asked Fraser if he had kept the bit of rag. 'Yes,' said the Q.M.G., and pulled it out of his pocket. 'Just see if it fits this,' said the spy, and, untying the end of his loin cloth, he matched the piece which had been torn from it. Thus the brave spy had fully proved that, on the previous night, he had taken his observations himself.' [This valuable note was written by Colonel Maude.—J. W. S.]

putting a slight upon him; to many there seemed a peculiar propriety in Outram's appointment, but still there it was; with whatever motive carried out, or by whatever circumstances justified, there was the thing, a supersession.

Illness was frightful. Cholera, dysentery, and fever were raging. A most accomplished and agreeable man, a Captain Young, occupied the next tent to me. He went down to dinner one evening at the hotel, which held on with comic pertinacity, and partook of some tinned provisions. The next morning he came out to early tea, but said he felt poorly, and would lie down. He died about noon, and was buried in the evening. An excellent linguist and manager of natives, it would have been his work, had he lived, to keep the road well open to Allahabad. He was to have been a travelling policeman. Sheehy, too, who came up in our tent, died of cholera. And the case of Brown was a very sad one. When we were at Banda, Mayne heard occasionally from Mr. Lloyd at Humeerpore. This was a place west of Banda, on the Jumna. Lloyd was there with an assistant, and two or more officers of a native regiment, one being Brown. He wrote with courage and submission, but without hope. They were in a pokey hole, whence they had no escape, and they had to wait for the outbreak. They kept a boat at the bottom of the garden, and all stayed together. One day they were at luncheon—the crisis came. Shouts in the air; the noise of feet; muskets firing; the heavy hum of a crowd. They ran down the garden, and took to their boats. Towards night, I think, they put in to shore. They were surrounded. Lloyd and another were carried back. Two of them, Brown was one, got across the water, and into the fields and jungles. At length Brown was separated from his companion, and, half dead with hunger and fatigue, was taken in by a kindly Zemindar. When Havelock passed up towards Cawnpore, at one halt Brown was sent into camp in a litter. He was lame and lacerated, and in a strange condition of nerves, in which he found speech difficult; but being a strong, naturally fleshy, and well-grown young fellow, he soon recovered, but only to die of cholera. There was another officer, who, it was understood, was engaged to a young lady, then amongst the besieged in Lucknow, so that he was fighting like a Paladin to recover his Princess from the Saracens. But it was not to be. The barracks got inundated one day, and, curiously enough, we observed that several who took off shoes and stockings and paddled about got cholera. Alas! the Paladin was amongst them. There was the gloom of the weather, gloom of the news—for Delhi was not taken—gloom of death; we thought the soaking neem trees smelt of the blood of the massacres; but hope springs eternal in the human breast, and a paper was handed to me one morning, headed *Cawnpore Summer Race Meeting!*

Brown's arrival had, at the time, created much interest, but, in due course, two much better known refugees arrived —Mowbray Thomson and Delafosse—and with them Private Murphy and Gunner Sullivan, who had shared their fate. Delafosse was then a pale, wiry, young man; Thomson, though his ample ruddy beard showed maturity, had the bright face and laughing eyes of an undergraduate in his first term. Both struck me very much in one way: they took the events which had happened to them, events almost surpassing the most romantic adventures of fiction, as if they were ordinary circumstances to be looked for in the day's work of life. Some years after, a London banker, sitting next me at dinner at Cambridge, began talking about Thomson, and asked me if I had met him. I told him I had seen him every day of my life for a year or two. "Well," he replied, "I met him in London once, and I shall never forget an answer he made to a question of mine. I asked him: 'When you got once more amongst all your countrymen, and the whole terrible thing was over, what on earth was the first thing you did?' 'Did?' cried he, 'why, I went and reported myself as present and ready for duty.'" The wonder created in the banker's mind was exactly what arose in mine. It did seem strange, indeed, that men should be able to resume ordinary life, after such an episode, as if nothing had happened.

There must, of course, be more of this kind of thing in the world than one would suppose. For instance, when one comes to think of it, probably the next morning after the earthquake at Lisbon, those who had any crockery left made coffee as usual. Thomson, being a handy fellow, able to turn his hand to any trade, was employed on the entrenchment, and might be seen rushing after the coolies any morning, as if he had been born to it.[1]

So the idea of the races was really a good one, for the men wanted cheering; and, as a mere sanitary measure, some small excitement was necessary. We often found horses. They had, perhaps, been taken by Zemindars, and

[1] Sir George Trevelyan charmingly said of him: "This officer did his best to lose a life destiny seemed determined to preserve, in order that England might know how, in her exceeding distress, her sons had not been unmindful of their ancient honour."

let loose, for fear of the condemnation involved in possessing them, should discovery be made. There was, too, an old Arab merchant in Cawnpore, who replied to all inquiries as to his loyalty by stating that he was a Freemason; and he in some wonderful way got hold of horses every now and then. Amongst the officers who had come up with the 84th was one named Blake, who was Petulengro, as George Borrow has it, or master of the horse-shoe. Everything connected with the noble quadruped delighted him, but especially driving. Palliser and Simpson,[1] the two Cavalry officers whose regiment had melted away, lived close to me on the glacis, and, Blake consorting with them, I was referred to as to the feasibility of a four-in-hand for the races. I have mentioned the Nana Narain Rao. Though he had come in to pay his respects to General Havelock, he had gone back to Bithoor, relying, I suppose, for personal safety on his high Brahminical rank, and being anxious to defeat any attempts of his brothers, who were declared by him to be rebels, to get away family property. But the last time Bithoor was filled with Sepoys and malcontents, he really did get harrassed, and had his little daughters taken from him, so that when Havelock cleared the place he determined to come into Cawnpore. He was fond of

[1] Simpson accompanied Captain Gordon in a steamer expedition to Bithoor (August 8), and amused us afterwards with an account of his adventures. They had two six-pounders and a mortar with them; but the shore offered much shelter to the rebels, and amongst them were many men of the 42nd Regiment. Thus protected, the enemy kept up a very sharp musketry fire. In coming back, the steamer ran aground, and could not be moved all night. Fortunately, the sand-bank was pretty well in the middle of the river. The Sepoys brought guns down to the spot; but in the morning the strong current carried the boat through.

horses, and had a great deal of harness; and, one of the merchants offering to lend me a barouche with a high box, and a very fair pair of horses, Narain Rao turned out the leaders, and found some four-in-hand traces and reins. So Blake was set up with his drag. He could drive anything, and kept the four together as if they had always run in a team. But we wanted a cornet to give completeness to the equipage; and I was told of Bandsman Jones, who had been hidden during the entrenchment troubles by some compassionate villager. He had belonged to one of the native infantry regiments, and was a tall, slimly built Eurasian. So I sent for Jones; and, when he came, I said: "Mr. Jones, I want you to go to the races with me." He said he should be delighted. I told him I also required him to contribute to the hilarity of the occasion by playing on the horn. And to this I understood him to agree, too. "Oh, he could play, certainly, some lively air which would be approved." So the drag was quite ready on the morning of the races. And Jones appeared, but without his horn. We inquired the cause of this omission. "I do not play on the cornet," he replied; "but I shall give some nice music on this," producing that pensive instrument—the flute. We were prepared for most emergencies, but a four-in-hand accommodated with a flute-player was too much for us, and we were compelled to explain to the obliging Jones that there were pastoral associations connected with the flute which rendered its introduction into the more robust scenes of horse-racing unsuitable.

The races served their purpose of rousing the men from the low spirits into which the prevailing sickness had thrown them. One of the best horses, the best I think, was an Arab that had come with us all the way from Banda, under the guidance of Dr. Clark, and either then, or shortly afterwards, Major Stirling of the 64th appeared on the handsomest Arab I ever saw. It was a bright bay, not very large, but beautifully shaped, and had the most high-caste and lovely head ever carried on shoulders. After the sad events of November, it became the property of Mowbray Thomson, and "Adonis," as he was called, developed into quite one of the notorieties of the station. I remember another little scene at the races. General Havelock was of course there, with his son and Colonel Fraser-Tytler, and, just as the party were passing a tent, a most extraordinary figure emerged. He was dressed in a wild billycock hat, had a huge spotted belcher tied round his throat, and was muffled in a vast dressing-gown. He looked for all the world like the man in the circus who has a great number of suits on, and gradually strips till he comes to flesh-coloured tights, and a blue ribbon securing his hair. The eccentric figure made as if it would address the General; and, as the figure, in addition to its own oddity, led a bull-dog in a string, the spectacle was very funny. It ended by some of his comrades dragging him out of sight. The hero of this little escapade was a young fellow in the Madras Fusiliers, who was much liked, a very well-informed man, agreeable and spirited, and one who would certainly have got on. Indeed, there had already been some talk of the V.C., but the mischief was, he could not keep away from the fire-water, and, before the advance to Lucknow, he was obliged to send in his papers. When it was too late, he carried out total abstinence with complete success for a period, and got employment in the Commissariat, or some other department; but, in the course of time, feeling somewhat out of health, he went down country in the hope of getting home. Unfortunately, he met one of his former kidney at Benares, and they had what is euphemistically called a "wet evening." The ex-Fusilier retired to bed in the Dawk bungalow at a late hour, and the next morning was found dead.

Bruce was invested with full powers by the Government, and with the assistance of Baba Bhut's papers, and the evidence of informers, got the names of many persons who had joined the Nana, or, at least, had acquiesced in his rule, had paid him complimentary visits, or had sent him presents. One of the informers was a tall, stout man of the sweeper caste; and though Bruce had certainly made him no kind of promise of immunity, he had taken so prominent a prosecuting part, that he quite thought himself established as a Government agent. It came out, however, quite clearly that he had jewellery in his possession which had belonged to some of the lady prisoners. I have all along supported the idea that there was no mutilation of our unfortunate countrymen and countrywomen before death, because there was no proof of it; it was not likely; and it seems such gratuitous self-torture to suppose a thing which everyone would desire to be untrue. But some mutilation after death may have taken place; and in one visit to the garden in which the well stood, shortly after our arrival, I found a hand under a bush, which I took, by the slenderness of the bones, to have been that of a female. The busy ants had made all clean and white, and the hand looked like a plaster cast in an anatomical museum. It lay on the direct road to the well; and when I heard of the jewels, it at once occurred to me that it was probably severed for its rings. Bruce was pledged to no leniency; and he would not forgive this stout sweeper, who, I make no doubt, had actually joined in the massacre. He and his mates had served as hangmen in disposing of some of the rebels whom Bruce had tried. And now his own hour was come. His mates turned on him, when ordered, with a readiness that must have been very bitter to him, and led him, bound and trembling, to the scaffold on which he had himself stood so often as executioner. I was with Umurnath in the verandah of a little house which he had to pass, and, seeing me, he cried at the pitch of his voice, "*Dohai Collector Sahib*," and entreated his guardians to allow him to stop and speak to me. But they were inexorable, and hurried him to his fate.

That I may not have to return again to this disagreeable subject, I will add a word or two about executions. As a rule, those who had to die died with extraordinary, I was going to say courage, but composure is the word; the Mahomedans, with hauteur, and an angry kind of scorn; and the Hindoos, with an apparent indifference altogether astonishing. When the *London* steamship went down, south of the Land's End, the Captain—that noble fellow who, when offered a seat in the boat, said, "No, thank you, I will stay with the passengers,"—about noon assembled all who could come into the saloon, and gave notice that he thought the ship would keep afloat till two o'clock. One who escaped related that, in answer to this notice, an old gentleman appeared at about half-past one having arranged his dress for a journey, strapped his wrappings together, and put his money into a girdle. Even in that supreme moment the Captain could not restrain a smile. Some of the Hindoos treated death exactly as if it were a journey. One man, positively under the shadow of the fatal tree, with only three or four minutes to live, when his waist-cloth was searched (for the benefit of his friends) did not object to one or two articles being taken out, but demurred, peevishly enough, to giving up a few apples of the jujube tree. Of all who had to meet their end, I only remember one who died craven. He was a Mahomedan, and, whether his memory was charged with upbraiding circumstances, or whether he had never looked the subject fairly in the face, when it really came to the last scene, he was unprepared to go through it. He declared that he only nominally belonged to Islam, but was at heart a Christian; that he was prepared to eat pork and drink wine, in order to show how sincere his conversion was; and that he thought little or nothing of Mahomed. All this not availing, he grovelled on the ground, screamed, cried, and piteously entreated for life. He would betray his cause, would turn informer, would deliver hundreds, now in security and honour, to the shambles—life, only life! And the poor wretch, fainting and foaming, had to be lifted within reach of the rope.

One more of these dark scenes and I have done. It was after Peel with the Naval contingent had arrived, and late one afternoon, verging on sunset, Bruce had tried with great patience, if with little emotion, a Mahomedan who was a person of some consideration. It was not uncommon for officials, who had made money by some of the more than doubtful methods in vogue during the administration of the King of Oudh, to withdraw across the boundary with their gains. There was consequently at Cawnpore a small *coterie* of families, not necessarily of good birth, who had, for periods of greater or less duration, occupied positions of eminence about the Lucknow Court, and who, enriched by the emoluments or opportunities of their office, had settled in this frontier city of our territory. Here, with the vices often enough gathered in the emasculate capital in which they had made their fortunes, they fell gradually into narrower circumstances, partly through extravagance and partly through increase in numbers. The head of one of these families, a man who, I was told, had in former days hardly ever left his own house, was considered by Bruce to have been shown to have taken an active part in aid of the rebel Government which had prevailed at Cawnpore. He was believed to have especially attended to the wants of one of the batteries directed against Wheeler's entrenchment. And it ended in his being condemned. Passing near the place of execution, and observing a considerable tumult, I thought I had better go and see if I could, in any way, help to keep order. The confusion arose from the interest taken in the man, which had drawn a crowd of Mahomedans from the city, as also from the accidental presence of a body of sailors. When I got there I found these latter very anxious to take the executive portion of the proceedings into their own hands, but a little explanation induced them to resume the character of spectators. The condemned man was timid, but not without self-possession. He said something which I understood to be that Jesus was a forgiving prophet; and that even if he had committed a fault, it should be overlooked for the sake of Jesus. He spoke very low, and it was not easy quite to make out his words. But the sacred name was certainly mentioned more than once. When all was over, one of the sailors got up on a wall to address the public. The speech was in English, and therefore failed of effect in any way, but it was a singular harangue. The following may represent it: "First of all, understand," he said, "that you are all rascals! And now you have seen a rascal die. But what is one rascal? My opinion is that not only one black rascal should be hung, but every black rascal in the country! And then you black rascals would learn how to behave yourselves." This view of the question was at least free from obscurity, though it was difficult to conjecture whence the regenerated remnant could arise. Balzac, in recording an axiom of "La Bohème," added: "*Le texte de cet article est plus vigoureux; mais comme, selon moi l'esprit en est faux, je ne tiens pas à la lettre.*" And I may make the same remark with regard to the funeral oration of our Naval friend.

Though sickness was still prevalent, the men were recovering their spirits. Large reinforcements were known to be coming, and an onward movement under more favourable circumstances was in prospect. The officers, too, were full of spirit and impatience. At a dinner got up at the conclusion of the races, Olpherts spoke with great animation and effect; many leaped to their feet, and looked as if, under the enthusiasm they felt, no task would be too great for them. One morning, the first of September, after breakfast, a messenger brought word that some Sahibs had arrived in a boat. I hastened from my tent to the river bank, and found George Probyn (brother of Sir Dighton), his wife, two children, Mr. William Edwards, and Mr. Gavin Jones. They had been saved from the massacres at Futtehgurh by the kindly offices of a Zemindar. Edwards, indeed, did not belong to

Futtehgurh; but had, after many adventures, joined the Probyns. The lady, wonderfully brave and calm, and neatly dressed, too, notwithstanding all deprivations, stood on the bank, the soldiers attending to the children and trying to reassure them. There was, however, one subject that had to be carefully avoided; there were two children with their mother, but two had been left behind. Buried in ground close to the shed, which was all the shelter the Zemindar could safely give, they rested from their little joys and fears for ever. Mr. Edwards I knew well by name, but had never seen. Mr. Gavin Jones had a bad wound, which he had never been able to get attended to; and was obliged to carry his arm out of his sleeve.

Owing to the droll circumstance of friend Mahomed's adherence to his profession, the hotel was available for the new comers, and its seedy equipments seemed to them, of course, a dream of comfort and luxury. A curious physical experiment worked itself out. Edwards was of a mercurial temperament, capable of going through anything, whilst his nerves were braced by hope and expectation. Probyn, less excitable, looked in poor health from insufficient food. As soon, however, as he was restored to English diet, he picked up at once. But the other, when the tension was relaxed, was visibly enfeebled and worn down. A day or two after this arrival, there came another company from Calpee, Messrs. Thornton, Passanah, and Griffiths, Eurasian gentlemen in Government employment across the Jumna, who had gone through many dangers and annoyances. With them, too, was found a Mahomedan Tuhsildar, Gholam Hussain Khan, through whose fidelity their escape had been partly effected. He came to call, and I was much struck with his fine appearance and honest face. He was a bluff man, outspoken and frank; but a thorough specimen of the best type of Pathan. Some of his connections and acquaintances had gone against us; but I never could make out that he had even wavered. I told him at once that if he would wait patiently I would certainly find a post for him, and from that time we trusted each other, and I think it may be added that neither ever repented of the confidence.

Hardly anything could be done in the district; several, indeed, of the Zemindars wrote and said they would bring in money when the roads were safe; and one or two offered to try and keep order in their own neighbourhood. It was necessary, however, of course, to have some guarantee that they were really loyal. After the mishap at the first Thana established, caution was necessary, especially as Bruce had had a similar misfortune at Bithoor. It had been represented that this place also required to be under military control; and Bruce had been directed to send some of what he called his sweeper police. As far as, in some measure, disregarding caste goes, the idea was sound; but the engagement of exclusively low-caste men was, perhaps, carrying things too far. Curious adventurers turned up from time to time; and a tall, well-built Hindoo had appeared, who spoke English admirably, and had attached his fortunes to those of Bruce. Men were required to go to Bithoor, and I was sitting one afternoon with Bruce, who was enlisting volunteers. They had to give some reference, and this Hindoo questioned them with great acuteness. At length one man was brought up, and the Hindoo said: "This fellow relies on his face, and the reference is very unsatisfactory. I had better tell him to pack?" A person capable of conducting business in so lively a manner was not to be overlooked, and when the Thana was established at Bithoor, he was sent over to preside. But he was a regular scamp; and, after a day or two of business, determined to have a frolic; and so sent for wine and dancing girls, and had the Thana laid with carpets, and lighted up, and devoted the night to music and the flowing bowl. A spy, however, sent word to the other side of the river, and a party of Sepoys and rebels got across, came quietly up, and made an attack on the revellers in the small hours. All outlook and precautions had been neglected, there was an attempt to get to arms, but of an ineffectual kind—a fight took place—several were killed. Our lively friend had taken too much to escape, or indeed to be fully aware, perhaps, of what was going on. He was murdered, and his body thrown into the street.

One duty, which was by no means an unpleasant one, was the endeavour to keep open communications with Agra. We always found men who were willing to take the risk. They would, perhaps, not have been killed, if the letters had been found; but very probably mutilated. Later on, several of our adherents had their noses and hands cut off. The letter was written on a small piece of paper, and put into a quill; the quill, again, sealing-waxed at the end, or sewn into a little case of wax cloth. The object was so small, it could be popped into the hair or held behind the teeth in an emergency. One of these tiny scrolls brought the last handwriting of Mr. Colvin. Mr. (afterwards Sir William) Muir was the best correspondent. Sometimes Neill got notes direct from Delhi; these were generally in French. As the communication was fairly open to Calcutta, friends of those in the fort at Agra began to write overland, *via* Cawnpore.

When a good number were collected, Umurnath and I set about making them as small as possible, and then got a Kossid to dress as a travelling beggar. A miserable pony was procured for him. It had to be a mere bag of bones, and yet to walk to Agra. We could not give it corn, as that, doubtless, would have brought on inflammation of the stomach; and when turned loose on the fresh grass, its old teeth produced effects much like those following the mowing of a lawn by a person unacquainted with the art. On this sorry brute was bound a most moth-eaten and weather-stained pad, tied roughly with a rope. But deeply inserted in the mouldy lining were the overland letters taking comfort and refreshment to many a heart. We daubed the Kossid into a filthy and odorous fukeer; and giving his Rosinante a meal of some kind of thatch, the cereal it most affected, we started Her Majesty's Mail on its journey. It arrived, I am glad to add, in perfect safety.

Notwithstanding all drawbacks, the time was not unpleasant. The works at the entrenchment were pushed forward, and at length presented the appearance of a strong little fort; those who lived there had constant intercourse with the Force, occupying the barracks to the east of the town. We lived from day to day, receiving and discussing any item of news that turned up; but I suppose, from a military point of view, the position was anything but reassuring. The black cloud at Gwalior still lay, with its presages of storm, on the horizon. But it might move any day. There were also symptoms of disturbance on the Ganges, between Cawnpore and Allahabad; and an attempt seemed threatened to occupy Futtehpore, or some other place near, so as to intercept communications. The steamer, which had been so wonderfully useful already, was sent down the river this time, and did good work in capturing boats and rendering crossing more difficult. Notwithstanding all, however, the enemy actually did cross, and endeavoured, as Outram was advancing, to occupy his rear, and cut off his communications. How that General gave them a blow, which sent those that escaped flying back into Oudh, is a matter of history. Sir James Outram arrived on the 16th of September; and, of course, his coming made a great change in our comparatively small society. The 5th Fusiliers, the 90th Light Infantry, appeared on the scene. The 64th was largely reinforced. Celebrities were there: Eyre, who had done such wonders at Arrah, and others—and there was the Bayard himself.

I felt somewhat nervous on entering a room in the large house on the bank, where he had taken up his quarters—a little out of conversation, as one does find oneself when first in the presence of a person of whom one has heard much. The kindly face, the friendly hand extended, the entire absence of stiffness, or self-consciousness—reminding me greatly, in this noble and natural simplicity, of Mr. Thomson—soon brought re-assurance. He took the trouble to show me a map of Lucknow, and to explain some of the difficulties of reaching the Residency. And never neglecting an opportunity of encouraging what he thought was right, he told me he had not failed to observe how harmoniously all efforts for the objects in view were working together. There was a bridge of boats[1] building at a

[1] Lord Canning kindly had a private letter written to me about this bridge. He was very pleased when it was finished. The flautist, Jones, was appointed toll-man.

tremendous pace across the Ganges; and, of course, friend Umurnath and I had had to assist as much as possible with coolies and materials, and so on.

And now for a few days all the bustle, noise, and animation of a moving camp were around us. I met some whom I had known before. Colonel Cooper of the Artillery was one. A fine, tall, stalwart man, he had been once chosen, some years before, for *Front de Bœuf* in "Ivanhoe" tableaux, and I remembered consultations as to his dress. The Artillery was now put entirely under him, and in the advance he was a Brigadier. Proud of the opportunity, come at last, of prominently distinguishing himself, and ardent as all the rest, there was about him, or I thought there was, a certain repose, a certain silence at times, which struck me then as foreboding. Does coming death cast a shadow? I recollect General Neill saying one morning: "Come out of the sun; I do not want to expose myself—*before my time.*" The last words were spoken with a smile and a look of his usual dauntless manner, but not untinged with sadness. When I heard of his fall at the Gateway, the words and the look returned to me with painful vividness. And here, while I am with General Neill for the last time, let me add what pleasant remembrances I have of his kindness. A man originally of a self-confident character, excessively praised and flattered for acts indicative of firmness, it was natural he should be positive, and natural that he should be brusque towards those who in any way opposed him. But the notion that got into the newspapers, that he was overbearing to persons who were not of his own profession, and that he set his face against all attempts to re-establish merely civil institutions, was not only incorrect, but was contrary to the fact. I have said that the idea that there was the least want of unanimity between Sir John Grant and himself was absolutely untrue; and I can only add that, as a civilian at Cawnpore, I received nothing but cordiality and consideration from him. He constantly sent for me to hear news he had received; and when small packets reached me from Agra, I took them down to open in his presence, that he might be the first informed. In this way I read out Nicholson's splendid surprise march on the rebel camp at Nujufgurh, when the attempt was made from Delhi to get to the rear of our Force. It was received, as may be supposed, with a genuine enthusiasm by Neill. He was very kind to the soldiers, and attentive to their wants and comforts; and those officers whose appointments brought them into daily intercourse with him were all attached to him. General Outram, as soon as he reached Cawnpore, issued the memorable, and it may surely be added, extraordinary order, in which he left the chief command with Havelock. That it did honour to his heart, no one, of course, could dispute. But there was no question of Outram's heart. He was known to be the most generous man alive. The difficulty that exercised many military minds was of a different kind. Can an officer, entrusted with a task by the Queen, make that task over to another person? I have mentioned, further on, what Outram himself said on the point, in a room where I happened to be present, after having plenty of time to think over the past events of 1857.

And now, we who were to remain, stood on the river bank. From the same spot, a day or two before, we had seen small parties of the enemy leaping and scuttling as the shrapnel fell near them. A hero on an elephant had displayed undignified anxiety to get beyond the reach of shells, when he had inadvertently come within their range. Outram reined up his mottled roan horse on the mound where we were—the same which carried him soon afterwards in the charge with Barrow's Cavalry. He was bearded and sat erect, as if his youth had returned. The long array wound down to the water, and slowly crossed over into Oudh. Men of history were there: Havelock and Napier, Neill and Eyre; and many others. The pageant passed us; and by night-fall the troops were spread out on the opposite shore. Next day the heavy guns were taken over—a task of some trouble, of course—and on the 21st of September, early in the morning, amidst one of those downpours that mark the end of the rains, we heard the cannonading at Mungulwar.

VIII

ANXIOUS WEEKS

THE throb of guns, ever and anon, was all that told us of the host growing more distant hourly. We seemed to be a very small party when left alone. Our new Commander was Colonel Wilson of the 64th, a type of the soldier now passed away. Well-bred, comely in appearance, of active and regular habits, a great stickler for all the traditions of the Service, a disbeliever in modern ideas of warfare, an opposer of reforms, he was on a small scale what Sir George Brown was on a large one: but withal a man of kindly disposition, and with much of the courtesy of an elder chivalry about him. The Probyns and Mr. Edwards had departed, and Probyn had been appointed magistrate of Futtehpore. But we had a few additions to our small society. Though death had, in the earlier autumn, been very busy amongst the troops, and there was more than one somewhat secluded spot, where the simple, rounded heaps told of the unknown but not inglorious brave sleeping beneath, no minister of religion had appeared to console the last moments of those who fell for their country, But with the last reinforcements a Baptist minister, a Mr. Gregson, came up, as also a priest of the Latin Church, Father Conti. The Nonconformist was a man of considerable ability, and free from sectarian prejudice; indeed, he often dwelt with satisfaction on the circumstance that he had never been called upon to sign any especial "Credo," though of course his general acquiescence in what is understood as Christian orthodoxy was pre-supposed and actually existed. The priest was a Capuchin missionary, who had temporarily given up his particular vocation under the emergency of circumstances. He brought with him several copies of the Rheims Testament, and some of these reached Protestants also who were devoid of all religious books. I received, too, a coadjutor in a Mr. George Benson, a man of much ability, who had got himself appointed to Cawnpore, to relieve in some measure a great anxiety felt for relatives who were shut in at Lucknow.

Bruce's position, without the support of General Neill, was, in a degree, anomalous; but a commission he had received to correspond with Outram strengthened his independence. Still, of course, he was under the orders of Colonel Wilson, and it was not part of the latter's idea of military administration to exercise any divided authority, so that circumspection was necessary. As for the position of civilians, the old disciplinarian took an early opportunity of telling me that all the difficulties of India had arisen from weak attempts at holding the country by other than military tenure; and that, for his own part, he was quite unprepared to recognise any other functions than those under his own control. I could not help thinking of Balzac's *Prince de la Bohème*, who refuses to admit that a person with so unchivalric a name as Godin has any perceptible status, "*Godin! cela n'existe pas, vous n'êtes rien, Godin!*" But, as soon as it was perceived that official annihilation, if theoretic only and not practical, was not objected to in any way, all resentment evaporated, and we became very friendly. Sometimes I got little scrolls from Agra, and the Colonel much liked their being read to him first, as, of course, it was proper they should be. The only difficulty was the telegraph, because Mr. Grant had decided that from time to time telegrams should be sent to him. But, however, Bruce played into my hands, and an opportunity occurred, of which I was glad to avail myself, when something in return could be done for him. The fall of Delhi, though it created an immense sensation throughout the country, of course let loose a vast body of ex-Sepoys and ruffians who started South. And some little time after Outram had gone to Lucknow, we heard that a considerable force of native troops was advancing down the Grand Trunk Road, they being determined, as it was said, to die in the *Cawnpore khet*, or fields of Cawnpore, where many of them, perhaps, were born. Bruce was anxious that something should be done to prevent this force actually advancing to within "measurable distance" of Cawnpore. But the Colonel had received strict directions, and shook his head. And as a diversion seemed to him advisable, to relieve himself of hints and suggestions, he took the opportunity of a convoy, starting for Alum Bagh, to appoint Bruce to take charge of it. Bruce galloped over to my tent in consternation, for it did not suit his book, in the least, to leave Cawnpore; and yet, of course, he had to obey the Commanding Officer. So, on an understanding, I went over to call on Colonel Wilson, and gradually worked the conversation round to Bruce. If I had said a word of remonstrance, I should certainly have been asked to walk out; but I merely spoke in the most general way of Bruce's position;

said how useful he was making himself to Outram, by keeping kossids on the road, and how he had now got the threads of communication in his hands, which another person would find it difficult to take up. And, moreover, I dwelt on the point that General Neill had obtained special orders for Bruce to remain at Cawnpore. All this was said quite casually, as if it had no bearing on present events, and Bruce himself also wrote in the same casual way. In the evening Wilson sent for Bruce, and said: "On second thoughts I scarcely think I can spare you." Bruce was a man who was confident if he thought he was right, and so, no sooner was he relieved from fear of extinction, than he began hammering again at the expedition. I find no notice of it in Malleson; but all the same the expedition came off. Wilson, with a handy little body of troops, and two guns, and accompanied by Bruce, went two marches up the Delhi road, and drove the rebels out of a village they had just reached. They fled towards the river, and he pegged into them as they were crossing, and came back with his object effected, and in high spirits. Stirling, of the 64th, commanded whilst he was away. The convoy I have mentioned as nearly blowing Bruce's candle out is not remembered without sadness. George Benson, who had recently, by the way, given a little dinner at the Hotel, on his birthday, was constantly anxious to get nearer Lucknow, and he wanted leave to go with the convoy. On a point of this sort Wilson was all complacence. It seemed to him about as important as if a black beetle had desired to crawl along the road in the wake of the guard. Benson went and hung about the Alum Bagh, undergoing many hardships, till Sir Colin came through. Then he pressed on to Lucknow, which he had so earnestly desired to reach, and was shot dead at the attack on the Secunder Bagh. Being in no recognisable position, I do not think his name was ever mentioned; but he was a brave fellow, and had he done under orders what he did for affection, he would not have filled such an unnoticed grave.

The rains up-country generally finish, at the latest, by the first week in October, and, though the sunshine is very intense, yet mornings and evenings are balmy, the light golden, and the distances dream-like with the luminous haze. Rising very early on the morning of the 26th October, and accompanied by the faithful Azim Ali, I cantered on the soft side of the Delhi road, as we called it (for that had been the place our minds had dwelt on so long), and after a mile or two, fell in with the van of a large force. I soon met George Campbell (afterwards M.P.), whom I did not know then, but who stopped to ask news, and presently afterwards saw three men riding abreast, two of them being Harington,[1] of the Legislative Council, and Herbert Harington, telegraphist. These were relatives of mine, and of course the meeting was pleasant enough. We had all of us been through trials; but we were quite well and hearty, and looked forward, not behind. The troops now entering Cawnpore formed the well-known flying column under Greathed, that had such strange adventures at Agra, but were now commanded by Hope Grant. This gallant officer, socially celebrated before as a musician and performer on the violincello, had at last found

[1] Afterwards Sir Henry Byng Harington, Member of Council, and appointed Lieutenant-Governor of the N.W.P. His medical man, however, would not allow him to fill the post.

the opportunity so long expected, so nobly availed of, of coming to the front. My especial Harington was at the Hotel, and we had plenty to talk of; indeed, everywhere the conversation was most interesting, stories of Delhi, stories of Agra, stories of the march, all full of romance. Herbert Harington was with his brother Hastings, the young Artillery officer to whom his fellow gunners by acclamation assigned the Victoria Cross, for siege operations at Delhi. There was a Cross to be given, and the officers were allowed to choose the recipient. This was a double honour: "for valour" from the Queen, "for worth" from his corps. The career of Herbert Harington so well illustrates the temper of the times, that I may be excused for briefly noticing it.

He was at Oxford pursuing his studies. The Crimean War came. Studies seemed derogatory at such a crisis, and he volunteered for service; but the authorities would only allow him to go out in the transport. He went out and worked hard at Kertch, and other places, came home in 1856 by Varna, Rustchuk, Ratisbon, and reached at last the old parsonage where he had been bred. But from Brussels to Wiltshire—26 hours—no commissariat but what three coppers could supply, so that glory did not prove a paying concern. Then he returned to Oxford and finished his college course, with a view to starting as a coach. But the charms of adventure had been tasted, and the quiet academical career seemed impossible. He must go somewhere. "To India," said O'Shaughnessy, "in my telegraph service, the finest service in the world." (This expression was, in a measure, hyperbolical.) So in the telegraph he came, arriving at Agra in the cold weather, and taking his sword off the roof of the dâk carriage, with the expression: "My old Crimean sword, I shall not want *that* again." However, the summer found him in the Volunteer Cavalry —only too glad to possess the old Crimean sword, and use it, too, in some very hazardous encounters. And so here he had turned up again as a telegraphist. The column stayed a very short time in Cawnpore, crossing over into Oudh, and following the host we had seen wind out of sight, and had traced a little further by their guns. Harington went down to Calcutta to take his seat in the Legislative Council; Herbert went on towards Lucknow. But in the meantime reinforcements had been coming steadily up, and a constant stream of soldiers was upon us.

The merchants in Cawnpore had recovered their confidence, and would supply money in any amount; and my new coadjutor, Mr. James Power, who had come with the Agra column, and myself had a great deal of treasury work to do, paying the troops, etc. And though the district was still very disturbed, owing to certain causes—the chief being the absolute certainty that the Contingent was about to leave Gwalior—a belief began to spread that the tide was turning, and many communications from the Zemindars was received.[1] Gradually one or two of the principal farmers, within fair distance of the station, consented to become Sub-Collectors, and to gather in the

[1] One Zemindar was insolent. He sent word he had two guns, and if I would lend him a buffalo calf (meaning an elephant), he would forward them to our aid. I think he joined Kunwur Singh and disappeared. A repartee had been prepared, but was never delivered.

revenue. It seemed better that there should be no misunderstanding, and therefore, though it was certainly true that the Nana had taken some of the summer revenue, it was intimated, from the first, that such payments would not count, and must not be mentioned. The Eurasian gentlemen who came from Calpee all helped in what work there was, and one of them, Griffiths, was a fine rider, and would occasionally gallop out and visit some of our Zemindar adherents. Still, of course, it was the day of small things.

On the 3rd of November Sir Colin Campbell reached Cawnpore, and the next day James Power and I went to pay our respects. I had been told to expect rather a sharp fire of chaff, and therefore approached with an extra provision of equanimity. As far as mere manner went, we found the Chief rather elaborately polite, but he soon went off into sarcasm. He was very angry with George Campbell about an expression he had used in reference to one of the regiments, and he was exceedingly sore about the battle of Kujwa. Probyn, the magistrate of Futtehpore, had brought very prominently to the notice of Colonel Powell of the 53rd, the fact of a large body of rebels headed by Kunwur Singh, from Dinapore and Behar who had collected at a village to the south-west of the station, and Powell had taken upon himself to go out and attack them. He was killed, and the command fell into the hands of Captain William Peel, R.N., who, by a really brilliant movement, gained a complete victory. The enemy suffered severely, and three guns and three tumbrils were taken. But the battle had been fought against general orders, and Sappers had been used as common Infantry, and the Chief was displeased; angry even that Powell's attention had been drawn to the presence of the rebels, saying with great contempt that if "General" Probyn would mind his own business, it would be better for all parties. After this, a quarter of an hour with the calm, intellectual, diplomatic Mansfield, who gave some hints as to supplies and other points, in a very courteous way. He was a man with a striking face, dark thoughtful eyes, and a fine forehead.

A moment of trial had arrived for Sir Colin, whom it will be more convenient to call by the name he is now remembered by, that of Lord Clyde. At the very time a sufficient force had been gathered together to render the Relief of Lucknow certain, the black cloud that had lain, a sullen mass, on the horizon, sped on apace to the zenith. The Gwalior Contingent moved to Calpee. It was not known then, but it is known now, that it did so under the orders of Tantia Topee, the Mahratta, who, in the absolute dearth of able men produced on the rebel side, has been credited, somewhat too generously perhaps, with high gifts of generalship. Lord Clyde had to decide which task to undertake first: meet the Contingent, or go to Lucknow. He determined to relieve the long-beleagured garrison; and he left for the defence of Cawnpore a force of 500 men afterwards increased by Madras troops. But we were no longer under the command of Colonel Wilson; we had a new chief in the person of Redan Windham. He was quite a different type of man from the old regimental Colonel; he was handsome and debonair, very talkative, fond of a good story, dressy, and fashionable. But those who knew Colonel Wilson had grown to like him very much; he was not possessed of intellectual power, but he had a great deal of that worth which always makes itself felt. Just before he gave over command, he had mentioned to me the pleasure he had received from a letter assuring him of the health and safety of his wife. I asked where she was, and he mentioned a station in Western India. I observed that the countersign that evening was the name of the place, and it struck one forcibly enough as a casual proof of the quarter to which his thoughts naturally turned.

With a detachment coming from the East, Joseph Manuel turned up one morning, having gradually got round from Nagode, and being determined to follow the fortunes of his family friend, as he regarded me. His name for me was "my superior," a title which was found rather embarrassing, suggestive of Mr. Barlow, the moral tutor, and seeming to call for some weighty aphorism to be delivered occasionally, such as: "You see, my dear Joseph, that in the long run, virtue secures that self-satisfaction without which the most splendid accidents of life would be tasteless and unprofitable," etc. The girl, Georgina Anderson, too, a Eurasian of some sixteen or seventeen years, who had been badly wounded at Humeerpore, and taken charge of by a native doctor, was brought in. Bandsman Jones was found to have a wife, and with this family Georgina was placed, where she seemed to be as happy as possible. With the Force that came from Agra, an Engineer officer named Major Norman Chester Macleod had appeared, and to him the entrenchment was made over. He was a man who, perhaps, was not very good at office work, had an impatience of details, and very likely, in those endless returns so affected by the Government, was sometimes behind-hand. But he had, nevertheless, a streak of genius: seized on the weak points of the position, and made many remarkable improvements, which, when the hour of trial came, were highly appreciated. Having, in early surveying work, caught a fearful jungle fever, he was only able to sustain health by hydropathic appliances and a vegetable diet. It seems odd, but it is perfectly true, that a person who has strength of mind enough to adopt habits at variance with usage, in the certainty that they are beneficial to himself, does not escape the charge of eccentricity. And then to the observation, "What a good officer such an one is," comes the wretched depreciation, "Yes, but he is singular, he has a bee in his bonnet," and so on. Add to this that Macleod was of a very modest disposition. Years and years after the siege of Ghuznee in Lord Keane's time, it was found that Macleod was the man who laid the gunpowder against the gate in the night. I have heard him tell the story. Of course, after it was done, escape had to be immediate and precipitate. To him, all eagerness about the result, came suddenly lightning in his eyes, a numbness in his face, a confusion in his head, a forgetfulness of what he was doing and where he could be, dust in his mouth, blood on his hands. He had fallen head over heels into one of the ravines forming the rough ground around the fort. Death has removed him long ago from the scene, but the great ability and brilliant readiness with which he secured the safety of that entrenchment at Cawnpore seemed to show that in any independent and unembarrassed position (and he required this freedom), he would have become a distinguished officer.

I had a correspondent in Calpee, and news was obtained also through Messrs. Passanah and Thornton, who had come from that bank of the Jumna, and the tidings were bad enough. The town swarmed with soldiers, and preparations were in full vigour for crossing over the guns—two eight-inch howitzers forming part of the battery.

General Windham had had orders to send on all Infantry, and portions of regiments coming up to Cawnpore, towards Lucknow, and loyally he did it. I remember him on the other side of the bridge, where planks had been laid down in the sand, early in the morning, seeing parties off. Seated on a handsome horse, and full of spirits, he was a fine specimen of a hearty English soldier. But some heavy work was before him. There seemed to us who had remained all along at Cawnpore to have been so many starting and none returning. We could watch them moving along the bank, and at last reaching trees which hid them—and then this wretched Oudh engulphed them. Even when Windham got leave to retain some of the reinforcements, he sent on a small Force with guns on hearing of the taking of Bunnee bridge. I and my compeer, James Power, had moved our tents off the glacis, and got them placed in a rather better situation for easy reference, as people were often wanting money, and here we saw all the world. There were many officers who could not get up-country to their own corps, who were anxious to obtain employment somehow. A very old friend, Campbell Clark, of what was then the 2nd Bengal Fusiliers, turned up, and also no less a person than Coverley Jackson. He had held a very high post once at Lucknow, and thought he should be wanted again. A Zemindar had come one day, on a great, stout, rounded horse, such as you see painted in battle pieces, with a flowing mane, and he consented to sell it, and it was secured for Jackson's use.

And now came on the three momentous days, the 26th, 27th, and 28th of November. Even if I had the necessary power and knowledge, it would be out of character with these pages to attempt to produce an outline of the military events that crowded themselves into this short space. Malleson has given them clearly enough, only he does not seem to me to have borne in mind that though the movements of the enemy have become known now, they were very indistinctly followed then. Information as to the number of men or guns, in any particular place, could not be obtained with any accuracy; and Windham neither had, nor could have, much notion of what the rebel leader was really intending. The General had come into my tent on the 25th, and had been talking about what he meant to do. "I am certainly not going to let these fellows think we cannot act on the offensive," he said, and then he added, "these small engagements are awkward things, very little glory gained in winning them, and perhaps some valuable life is lost, and people say it was wasted." That night, on an intimation from Brigadier Carthew, he rode out to the camp, which had been formed on the Calpee road. The next day the battle took place near the Pandoo Nuddee, and a very brilliant affair it was, and completely successful, it must be remembered. The two howitzers of which we had heard were taken, besides a 6-pounder. As evening fell, several who had been present appeared, and we heard full accounts of the various incidents of the day. Early the next morning all was bustle and excitement—the troops had to stand to arms at 11 o'clock. The enemy, however, did not immediately appear, and we now know that the Force moving along the Calpee road was waiting for the advance of their comrades by the Delhi road. Those who had been living outside had some of them moved into the entrenchment, and we had made arrangements for striking our tents in case of necessity.

It was about noon, and I had gone into the entrenchment, and was standing with some officers on the grass, when we heard a heavy cannonade open from the direction of Nawabgunj, where the old civil station stood. From that moment, of course, all was excitement and confusion for hours. From time to time we got scraps of news which sounded encouraging. Carthew, as is well known, held the right and the approach from Bithoor successfully for a long time. However, we moved our tents and traps, and got them quietly into the entrenchment, so as to be prepared. And as the afternoon ended, the better things we had hoped for in the morning seemed passing away. Windham, on his way to see how the right was faring, received false intelligence that the entrenchment was being attacked, and sent orders for his left to fall back. There was a stampede amongst the few non-combatants still outside to get into the entrenchment, and then a very disorderly entry of military with bullock-drivers, camp-followers, and what not. Mowbray Thomson, Power, and myself, got up on a rampart and surveyed the scene, which was one of indescribable confusion. It is pleasant to think our soldiers do not withdraw well; they fortunately have very seldom to do it. And now night fell, and the whole Force which had held the left was inside the entrenchment. There were fires burning in one or two directions, and altogether it was rather an awkward time. The non-combatant portion of those enclosed had a large shelf of ground between the river and the bank assigned to them, and here the tents were placed close together. Just beyond was the Commissariat, and then a path led to a temple hanging over the water. There was an exit, by which a large house could be reached; this had been in a measure fortified, and was occupied by Windham and his Staff, Bruce, and others. We retired, as it grew dark, to the shelf where the tent was, and found all our acquaintances. Umurnath, the fat Brahmin, and Azim Ali, had made friends with some Commissariat people. Bandsman Jones and Mrs. Jones were close by, and Georgina Anderson, and Mr. Gregson, the Baptist minister. With the astonishing impassiveness of native servants, our table attendants had managed to cook dinner (as if a siege were a sort of picnic), and, like Swiveller's Marchioness, we made pretence of being very happy, and found it answer. Afterwards, being up in the open part, I caught a form I knew; it was Colonel Wilson. He was, of course, rather annoyed at what had happened, but still spoke with confidence of going at the enemy next day. "Straight at them, sir," he said; "it is the only way with these rascals. Good-night." "Good-night, Colonel." Sleep calmly, old soldier; it is thy last night on earth.

There was a determined little task to be done in the early hours of this night. One of the two big guns taken out had been left in the town, in the middle of the streets. There was no reason why the enemy should not have come into the city if they had liked, but they were cautious, and waited till the next day. This, of course, could not be ascertained then; and, therefore, the band that sallied forth to bring in the gun thought the project might be rather a hazardous one. However, after midnight it was in the entrenchment. The General had to make all his arrangements over night. Poor man! He had caught a frightful cold, and it had taken away his voice, so, when he desired to be especially emphatic, a wheezy earnestness was all that could be produced. I expect he never lay down or thought of sleep, and was only too glad when morning came, and he could set about retrieving matters. The next was a terrible day. We, non-combatants, had got an idea into our heads that Brigadier Carthew had been the hero of the 27th. He had been the only victorious one, and at night had stayed out, holding the Theatre. When we heard afterwards his exploits had received a reprimand, we were greatly astonished. He, it will be remembered, occupied a position on the right, but between this ground and the river there was sufficient space for the rebels to advance towards the entrenchment, and to post guns on a rising bank. When this was perceived, Windham sent word to Colonel Wilson, who was in command of the entrenchment, to sally out and occupy a place parallel with that held by Brigadier Carthew. The old Colonel, only too glad, doubtless, of an opportunity of carrying out the policy he had propounded the previous evening, issued forth at the head of his own corps, the 64th Regiment. On what a little matter serious issue may turn at a critical moment! Often and often since have I walked over the road he took. It ran in a line with the river for some little way, and then forked. One branch wound gently down below an old burial-place, the other descended more abruptly beneath rising ground, which, at the top, became quite steep.

If the Colonel had known the difference of the roads, and

had taken the one nearer the river, to his right, and, skirting the grave-yard, he would have come to a place whence he could have peppered the rebels at the guns they had pushed forward, without exposing his own men. It was, of course, not the least his fault; but he took the wrong turn, went down the more abrupt road, and so under the bank recently occupied by the enemy. His skirmishers climbed up the steep part, and got possession of the guns, but these could not be retained. Major Stirling, waving his sword, jumped across one of the guns, and shouted encouragement to the men embarrassed with the ascent. He was cut down by troopers coming up. The enemy rallied to the spot, six of the officers of the 64th were killed, and the endeavour to carry the height failed. In consequence of this, the mutineers closed up, and occupied the ground by the river, approached close to the entrenchment, and, from a sheltered position on the bank, opened a peculiarly misdirected fire on the bridge; and at a later stage made a feeble attempt to loose a fire-boat down the stream. Poor Campbell Clark had been brought into hospital, dangerously wounded; another friend, Parsons, I had seen go by with his arm all shattered, and I think it was late in the afternoon when, wandering near a gate of the entrenchment, I heard a voice reciting words, and looking round saw Moore, a chaplain recently come, in his surplice, moving slowly along. And then there passed, stretched on a hospital dhoolie, reverently covered up, and attended by a favourite Portuguese servant, all that was left of poor Colonel Wilson!

The sun was setting, or had set, when Power and I went down to see how the bridge was faring. It had never been in real danger, so inadequate had the attempts of the enemy proved. We crossed over, and were standing by the palisade at the end, when we saw a cloud of dust on the Lucknow road. This was soon recognised to be a small knot of horsemen, the central figure of which was peering across the water, as he turned his large-limbed horse on the quivering planks of the bridge.

The figure was Lord Clyde. When we went to bed that night, we felt that all real anxiety was at an end.

Early the next day Captain Peel took up a position on the Oudh bank, above the bridge, and pounded away into the enemy's left, with his big guns worked by the sailors. When the troops had passed over, and this occupied the whole morning, the convoy commenced to cross, and their transit was not complete till the next evening. To witness this transit was, as may be conceived, a spectacle full of interest, ladies and children and servants, and the wounded lying in their dhoolies, all went by in an apparently endless string. Colonel Malleson appears to think favourably of the abilities of Tantia Topee; but it is difficult to understand, if he was the "astute" leader he is represented, why he never attempted to interrupt the passage of the convoy. The river was comparatively low; above Cawnpore both banks were entirely in the hands of the Mahratta, and he had plenty of boats; why, then, did he not send Horse Artillery and Cavalry across to harass Lord Clyde's rear? But nothing whatever was done. The British Force went safely over, was stretched from our entrenchment far away along the east side of the canal; but the rebels occupied the town, and their left, having the shelter of trees and old houses, was pushed close up to the entrenchment.

Standing at the ascent from the bridge, as the convoy passed, many familiar faces were recognised. One or two of the wounded had themselves carried on to our shelf in the entrenchment; amongst them, Colonel Fraser-Tytler, who had been such a type of activity; he had a nasty wound, and was quite helpless. The younger Havelock also—by this time, indeed, alas! the only one—was down. We could get out now to the east, not simply as before to the fortified house where Windham was, but on to the plain. Indeed, you could drive. The convoy was behind the camp, and in comparative quietude. I went to call on Mr. Martin Gubbins, and saw his wife and sister-in-law, who, with that extraordinary calm courage English ladies possess, did not give any idea of having been through a frightful siege. The sight of children again was very pleasant, and they, true to their character, were wholly absorbed in their dolls, or some sort of knotted handkerchief which passed as such, or perhaps an empty sardine-tin drawn by a string, and enjoyed the cheerful weather, without thought of Tantia Topee, or any other bogie. When I returned to our tent, the noise seemed very great; but it was not continuous, only spasmodic; and perhaps some of it was, in a measure, unnecessary. If any of the enemy came within sight, there began a discharge of musketry on our part, which did not leave off for a long time. Why the rebels did not shell the entrenchment seems unaccountable. Occasionally a bullet came whizzing across, and one officer just sitting down to a cup of tea was killed in his chair. Once or twice, too, they began to fire round-shot at a central building used as an hospital, and considerable alarm was felt about the wounded. I tried to see Clark, but a doctor said: "He has only one chance—which is, quiet—pray let him have the benefit of that." We heard, too, that Parsons was very bad, and would lose his arm.

The convoy did not start for Allahabad till the 3rd of December, and then Lord Clyde was unwilling to move till news had reached him of its safety. The enemy occasionally became very audacious, mistaking, doubtless, the reason of the delay in attacking them. One day, when a friend and myself were in the large camp, they managed to get the range of Lord Clyde's quarters, and knocked all the breakfast things over in his cooking-tent. Not long before the end came, Bruce, who was in the fortified house, with Windham and his staff, sent a little note to me, to say that he was to have an appointment, and that after this crisis had passed, the abnormal state of things at Cawnpore would, of course, cease, and the military management of the city terminate, and that he was directed to make over charge to me. So I got out of the entrenchment by the little temple on the river side, and reached the house. That particular morning, the rebels had taken it into their heads that this house was a place of some importance, and, after some very bad shots, had got its range. The inmates had been driven out of the south verandah altogether, but the other side of the building was safe. As the house stood unevenly, there was on one side a small chamber partially underground, and Bruce said: "Go down there, and I will get pen and ink." I went into this hole, and, finding some bread and bacon on a shelf, was improvising a luncheon, when Bruce brought his papers. In this queer way I took charge. The incident did me a good turn afterwards, for —incurring some rather hasty criticism—I was enabled to represent the time and occasion as rude enough to excuse any executive deficiencies.

I have said that the enemy came close up to the entrenchment, on the extreme right. John Power, of my service, who had been distinguished in the early part of the Mutiny by holding on at Mynpoorie with his brother James, and De Kantzow, when all the others withdrew, had come down with the Agra column, and had gone on to Lucknow.

He was back again now, a fine tall man, who delighted in a kind of fantastic calmness which was very entertaining. At his invitation, Mr. Gregson, the Baptist minister, and I went one evening to visit the posts on this extreme right. Of course most of the way we skirted along the bank, which had been thrown up, and where at short intervals soldiers were seated, ready to start up and fire if occasion called. It was not one of the stormy intervals, and therefore, besides being safe, the walk seemed also quiet. But there were occasional spaces—patches lighted up with the shining moon, where one's figure came out very distinctly, and might have formed a good mark for anybody in the trees, or buildings near. Mr. Gregson, as a minister of religion, and I, as the father of a family, thought it advisable to cross these patches at the double; but nothing would induce our friend to accelerate his saunter. "What are you afraid of?" cried he. "Oh," I answered, wishing vaguely to justify the action, "I do not care about myself." "Then please to say," continued our imperturbable companion, stopping in one of the bright patches to dispute the point, "for whose sake you *do* run!" At the extreme end down by the river we came to the wall of a small shrine which had steps to the water's edge, and here palisades had been put by our people. It was very curious to hear the rebel Sepoys talking inside this temple, and it could be done without difficulty, for they were, in space, only a foot or two from the English soldiers.

The operations at Cawnpore are described by Tantia Topee in his journal, or statement, in the following curious words: "Having arrived at Cawnpere, there was a battle which lasted eleven days. After eleven days, the revolted army was defeated, and we all ran away." The idea of the long battle pleased the insurgents very much, for one of the Contingent being taken afterwards in a village near, and brought in, said to me: "We performed a great action, and the fame of it has probably reached Vilayut" [foreign parts]. So completely are precautionary measures misunderstood by Asiatics. Of course, it is easy to think what a source of anxiety the convoy was to Lord Clyde. However, at length, it reached Allahabad, and the General's hands were no longer tied. It is, I believe, a fact that the rebels had begun to doubt of success, and to anticipate that they would soon be attacked in earnest; for, before the 6th of December, some movement of return towards Calpee on the part of a portion of the Force had certainly commenced. Those who desire to know what occurred when Lord Clyde considered the proper time had come for clearing Cawnpore of the host that had invested it, will find the account clearly narrated in the pages of Malleson. Some of the reviews found his language too magniloquent, and thought a defence of Lord Clyde for "risking his centre" rather unnecessary, when, in point of fact, the rebels were quite unprepared with any plan for resisting the attack which they could scarcely have thought would not ultimately be made. But, at any rate, it is easy to see what really took place by reference to the map, and by following the statement. And this surely is something.

About nine o'clock a tremendous fire was opened from the entrenchment. Malleson speaks of a "great artillery duel." It was scarcely that, for every one remarked how slack the return was. And though the rebels certainly had no idea how soon their right would be forced, and their camp actually taken, just as it stood and had been tenanted, there is reason to believe they had fallen back from their extreme left. The batteries in the entrenchment were very interesting, being worked by different races, one by Sikhs, one by Madrasees, and so on. I had formed the acquaintance of one Madras Artillery soldier. He was a little chap, but wiry and strong enough. He spoke English well, and was, I suppose, a Roman Catholic. He said: "You have never seen, I dare say, a native soldier like me. We are much nearer the English than the fellows up here. There is very little difference; we can eat any meat we choose, and drink wine." "And fight, I suppose?" I said; "the English are thought to be very fond of fighting." "Oh, fight," he cried, "I should think so. We are just English over again, only a different colour."

That forenoon was certainly one of the noisiest conceivable, where we were. What took place need not be repeated here. Malleson has spoken very plainly about the events at the Subahdar's Tank; and friends of General Mansfield have found great fault with him for saying what he has said. Camp reports are not of much value, perhaps, by themselves; but where there is other evidence, they may be held corroborative. Certainly there was very much discontent felt. There was a sense of an opportunity lost. But no one seemed to think that any oversight had occurred. The words attributed to General Mansfield, when he checked the attack, were: "What is the use of intercepting a desperate soldiery, whose only wish is to escape?" The belief that this phrase was used, added to the singular expression in the despatch: "I could have taken the guns," leads to the idea that he did not think the *jeu* worth the *chandelle*, deciding that it was better to spare precious British life than destroy worthless mutineers. And if he could have been sure that the guns would be easily taken in pursuit, perhaps the forbearance would have been excusable; it would certainly have been intelligible. But we know that the guns were very nearly got away; for Sir Hope Grant, who followed up the enemy afterwards, says himself that he only just caught them. The Mutiny would never have been put down if calm calculations had prevailed at first; but circumstances were not desperate now, and perhaps it was thought that the time of the Nicholsons and Neills had passed. At any rate, Lord Clyde expressed not one word of censure. The return from the Calpee Road pursuit did not take place till late, so that matters remained, that night, in the entrenchment, pretty much as before; but the next day we began to move out, and were able to go into the city. It was difficult to prevent looting, and, riding into one lane, I found a knot of women in great trouble, who declared they had been made to give up their nose-rings and other jewels; and, moreover, that the culprit was in a neighbouring house. I went with them to find him, and behold! he was one of the new police, who, by simply showing his firelock, had gained complete submission from all parties. He had quite a handful of ornaments about him. Mowbray Thomson had succeeded Bruce in charge of this body, and he took very strenuous measures to prevent further misconduct, so this particular offender was flogged at once, and dismissed the force.

One incident, however, took place, indicative of the lawlessness which, of course, had a tendency to break out on such occasions; for which I was very sorry. There was a tent-maker, in the bazar, named Choonee Lal, a man who had throughout taken the British side very loyally, and had been of great service in many ways. Naturally handsome, he had by grain diet and simple habits obtained a certain look of benevolent content, which made one almost believe in that ideal goodness Krummacher and others have attributed to Indian sages. He was sitting, it appeared, on a charpoy, only half-dressed, and proposing to come up to camp, when he saw, near his house, two soldiers enter a shop, and compel its keeper to give up his money. Choonee Lal knew English perfectly, and spoke to the men, telling them they were protectors, not oppressors of the poorer citizens.

An aphorism so gentle might have passed, but he unfortunately added that if any officer knew what they were doing, they would be punished. This sounded like a threat, and the knowledge of English, too, was calculated to create some alarm; and so the two fellows turned on their monitor, and one of them, putting his musket absolutely against Choonee Lal's side, discharged it. The poor body, with face uncovered, and the pleasant smile still lingering in death, was brought to my tent by the murdered man's nephew, who was present when the event occurred—and a truly sad sight it was.

General Windham, to whom the circumstance was at once reported, was greatly moved, and interesting himself extremely in the inquiries which were set on foot, managed to have the men identified and arrested; and the case was afterwards brought to a successful issue.

We got out again into tents in an open space, and indemnified ourselves for any past discomforts; but we often afterwards visited the ledge under the bank, where we had all lived, hugger-mugger, for several days.

But the place was not quite free from unpleasant associations, owing to a circumstance which occurred during our occupancy of it. Mr. Gregson and I were present when a noisy crowd approached the bank overhanging the lower plateau, and we found, in the centre of it, two men being roughly handled by some sailors and others. They were really bullock-drivers employed by our side, and, having got wounded, were in search of medical aid. But being ragged chaps, and smeared with dust and blood, they were set down at once, by the lawless party with whom they had fallen in, as rebels. No remonstrance or explanation that Mr. Gregson or I could make was of any avail, and the unhappy fellows lost their lives, and were precipitated headforemost to the level below. The tumult and confusion prevented us from distinguishing the actual perpetrators of the outrage; and, under the circumstances, it seemed scarcely desirable to lay our information before the authorities against men we recognised as members only of the crowd—illegal assembly though it undoubtedly was.

IX

DUNCAN'S HOTEL

ON the 8th of December, Lord Clyde sent Colonel Hope Grant in pursuit of that half of the rebel force which had retreated northwards, with a view of crossing into Oudh. Grant caught them at the ghât, near Sheorajpore, and captured fifteen guns drawn by beautiful bullocks. A large mass of the enemy got away towards Calpee; but they crossed the Jumna, and though they kept up great excitement and disorder in the part of the district near the river, they never actually returned with any set purpose. Lord Clyde did not, however, leave Cawnpore till Christmas, and his camp was formed some way out of the town, on the north-west side.

We were, of course, free now to move, and to choose some locality suited to our wants, and a large house was occupied as the headquarters of the Civil Administration, not far east of the Canal. It was a many-roomed, rambling place, standing in a compound, with a small garden and trees near it, had once been used as an inn, and was called by the natives Duncan's Hotel. Here quite a new life began. I and my immediate coadjutors, Power and Henry Willock, with Mowbray Thomson as the head of the police, formed the nucleus of the establishment, and certain aggregations gradually took place. Dr. Tresidder, who had formerly lived at this station, was appointed Civil Surgeon, and becoming acquainted with what was going on in the hospital of the entrenchment, he learnt from us that two of the patients were especial friends. The day was actually fixed for Parsons to have his arm amputated; but Tresidder declared that if the case were entrusted to his individual care, he thought he could save the limb. Arrangements were accordingly made, and permission obtained; and Parsons and Clark—the latter, though better, was still in a ticklish condition—were removed to Duncan's Hotel, where, with better air, specially prepared food, and the constant attendance of Tresidder in the house, they both got quite well. Parsons retained his arm, and Clark gave up trying to recover his watch chain. They both lived for some thirty-eight years after these events, and died within a month or two of each other. Clark was wounded dangerously in the stomach, the bullet carrying in part of the chain of his watch, links of which came away one by one, leading to the mild pleasantry that he was delaying recovery in search of his lost property.

It was never known how many inmates the hotel contained, for besides all of us, including some Oudh men temporarily attached, visitors occasionally turned up, and there was a dinner in the evening, to which persons not living in the house sometimes came. Joseph declared that though hitherto repressed by circumstances, he possessed a native genius for catering. To him, therefore, was entrusted the commissariat; and though rather wasteful and extravagant, it must be admitted he kept the table well supplied.

At length at Christmas—the very morning before Christmas day—Lord Clyde started for Futtehgurh, and the force at Cawnpore was reduced to a small garrison again, under Inglis. The entrenchment of course formed a fort; but there was no occasion to withdraw within it any more. John Power, who, as has been mentioned, had come down from Agra, and had been to Oudh, was to go on with the Force proceeding to Futtehgurh, and assist in making any Civil arrangements possible, as he possessed the necessary powers. But when the troops were nearly at the end of the district, I got a letter from General Mansfield, saying that it seemed odd the Magistrate was not present to place establishments of police where the troops had passed through. So Mowbray Thomson and I started that evening, and, riding all night, reached the camp. I only stayed one day, for they had reached the limit of Cawnpore jurisdiction.

But I was very glad I went, because I saw the Chief in such a good humour. He was in Bruce's tent when I went in, was telling anecdotes, and as kind as possible. "You have heard of the Koh-i-noor, I suppose—a world-wide gem? I tell you, I, Colin Campbell, have had that stone in a box with me in the Punjab, as if it were a toilet article, and no one the wiser." All sorts of subjects he talked about, and was most pleasant. It was a slight craze[1] with General Mansfield that order ought to succeed immediately after troops had once marched through a part of the country. When Lord Clyde started up the Trunk Road, he sent Walpole by a kind of loop-line through the south-west of the Cawnpore district, and astonishment was expressed that pacification did not at once take place. But, besides

[1] See Appendix No. IV.

broken bodies of rebels appearing sporadically, in various directions, during the six months of anarchy many of the old landholders had expelled auction purchasers out of their villages, and kept up disturbances in the vain hope of staving off the evil day of restitution. It was impossible, therefore, to proceed otherwise than slowly, in getting matters straight; and confidence required time to establish itself.

As we came back from the camp we were received by a good old Zemindar, who had been in communication with me at Cawnpore, had entered upon the duties of a Sub-Collector, and had begun collections for us, under written orders sent to him. He had been obliged to fly before the Contingent, but he was back again, and occupied the Collecting House, having filled it with his own armed retainers. As I walked in amongst wild matchlock men, I could not but reflect how little the Board of Revenue would have dreamt two years before, of a Rajpoot chief with his clan in charge of one of the sacred temples of the Fisc. Amongst the frequenters of the dinner table at Duncan's Hotel was the Commissioner—not Chester, who had gone home, but another. He had done wonderfully well in his own district, and had just been promoted. His decision of character had so struck two influential natives that they would not let him out of their sight, had travelled with him to Cawnpore, and had even requested to visit our mess-room after dinner, that they might be near their ideal. We were, of course, very glad to see them, and as they dressed most handsomely, they embellished the scene, and came to be called the two kings. I soon found that our new superior officer did not altogether approve of the course I had taken at Cawnpore. He was justly proud of a service which he had unquestionably adorned, and he thought that I had done something to "lower that service,' and ought to have asked to be relieved in preference to co-operating, when the military conceived it necessary to organise police, etc. He told me, in so many words, that he could not have acted as I had done. Such questions seemed to me out of season in times of common danger and anxiety. I could only answer, however, that I did not regret what had occurred. But from holding the views that he did, it was perhaps natural he should come to regard me as too easy-going, and to advocate the substitution of some one of a sterner mould. And one morning he remarked to me, quite casually, that I was to go to Ghazipore, where I should find matters in a less entangled state. I certainly understood him to say that Mr. Grant thought the move advisable. But some latitude of expression should be allowed, perhaps, to a person having an unpleasant intimation to deliver.

It seemed very odd, but I did not fear Mr. Grant, because I knew he took in the real position of things at a glance, and was a just and self-reliant man. So I sat down at once, and wrote to Mr. Grant, describing the way in which I had taken charge from Bruce, and giving reasons why the district was still in a very excited condition, and how necessary patience was in expecting the re-establishment of order; and ended by saying that I had scarcely yet had an opening for showing want of capacity—or its contrary.

Mr. Grant wrote back at once, in autograph, that in his opinion more could not have been done than had been done, and that he could not agree that removal was necessary or would be right. The matter passed over, and was never, perhaps, of much importance. But I consider it only fair to myself to add that in due time everything came straight at Cawnpore; that there was never any remission of revenue—those who had paid the Nana had to pay again; and that when the Lieutenant-Governor, Mr. George Edmonstone, came round on tour in the cold season of 1859, he found the district as it was before the Mutiny, with the exception of a proper jail, which had to be provided later on. He approved of the plan of employing influential farmers to act temporarily as Sub-Collectors till confidence was quite restored; and he was kind enough to say he was quite satisfied with all he had seen.

It was curious that very shortly after the removal business, Mowbray Thomson and I got into the Calcutta papers for a feat of great alleged activity. News had been brought to Thomson that certain property belonging to the Nana, and possibly including papers, was in the custody of a Zemindar, who proposed sending it to its owner. So guided by another Zemindar, we made a night-raid on the village where the property was said to be. We formed a good body of armed men, and made a pounce on the place at day-break. We turned somebody's house upside down, and seized some property, a portion of which was claimed by a courtezan, said to have been a friend of Doondoo Punt. But afterwards, doubts arose as to the fidelity of our guide, who was thought to be influenced by spite. However, we did not kill anybody or burn anything, and we went through the exhilarating sensations of amateur dacoity without much harm done, and as it turned out, with a transient increase of reputation.

The horse that had been prepared for Coverley Jackson had played him a bad trick on the return from Oudh. It was an entire animal, and went neighing all over the place, and on one occasion when he punished it to keep it quiet, it reared suddenly up and fell back, breaking Jackson's leg. So there was he—lying with his broken limb in Bruce's house, now a hospital, and not far from him lay Napier—afterwards Lord Napier of Magdala—slowly recovering from his wound. Meanwhile, we were not without distinguished visitors at Duncan's Hotel. We had Mr. Layard, and very pleasant and entertaining we found him. He was then passing from the traveller and savant into a kind of tribune of the people, which latter career, as we all know, was arrested by diplomatic honours.

Besides Mr. Layard, we had one or two travellers, a gentleman who had volunteered for any kind of service, also one of the Grenfell family, and greatest of all, Dr. W. H. Russell, Special War Correspondent for the *Times*. Coming in one forenoon, before the start for Futtehgurh, I found a strongly-built man, of middle stature, with a bright eye and a merry smile, speaking with a slight Irish accent, and dressed in a frogged and braided frock coat. This was Russell,[1] and he promised to come to dinner, and we had a most merry evening, for, in addition to other accomplishments, he sang very charmingly in a social way, and gave us, "We will catch the whale, brave boys!" and, "O lave us a lock of your hair!" in splendid style, the choruses being organised with great effect. From that day he was very friendly, and frequently sent me accounts of different events in the Campaign, and I have a bundle of his letters,

[1] Now Sir W. H. Russell.

with plans of positions sketched with a pen.[1]
her little evening afterwards when Colonel
his Knighthood; then Russell came again,
is reputation as a *raconteur* and an amusing
companion, to everybody's satisfaction. It shows how the occupation of Special Correspondent has grown, when it is remembered that he was the only member of the Press actually present with the army, employed in recording the manner in which the Mutiny was finally dealt with. In seeing him at work, I remarked one gift which seems an especially useful one. He would be sitting, pen in hand, writing his diary, or what not. You entered. "I hope I am not disturbing you?" "Not the least; I am all ears; go on." You went on, told your tale, he listening and answering. You stopped. His eye dropped on the paper; his pen moved; he resumed the thread of his writing without difficulty, and with an unembarrassed continuity.

Théophile Gautier had the same faculty. Emile Bergerat records: "Je l'ai vu plus d'une fois, à la suite d'une visite d'étranger ou d'ami, reprendre, sans s'être relue, une phrase interrompue, souvent à la moitié d'un mot, et la poursuivre dans tous ses développements avec la même tranquillité que celle qu'il mettait à rallumer son cigare."

Inglis was a delightful man to have in command—pleasant-tempered, agreeable-mannered, attending to anything asked, giving it if possible—saying at once why it could not be given if he thought it unadvisable. And often, with the easily-amused nature of a boy, he would start some little project. The soldiers, we found, were getting liquor very easily, and he had heard that they distilled spirit in a

[1] See Appendix No. V.

village just opposite, in Oudh. So he asked me one day to come and look for it. We crossed, and got into a knot of little houses, and in an unlikely-looking out-house we found a still. Inglis was as eager as a schoolboy at a badger hunt, and shouted at the discovery. We had some people with us, and we encircled all the villagers we could find with a rope, and brought them over the water to frighten them, setting the still on fire; and this, spreading to others we had not seen, made a clean sweep of the smuggling hamlet.

A man came in one night to say the jailer was afraid of the prisoners, and Henry Willock and I got up to go and see about it. As we rode down, we saw a man in a cloak on horseback moving through the dark, accompanied by companions. It was Lord Clyde, starting for his celebrated attack on Lucknow.

One morning, at the time of the advance on Lucknow, a tallish man, with yellow hair, a pale, smooth face, heavy moustache, and large, restless, and rather unforgiving eyes, came into my room at Duncan's. He looked at me in a stony way, and then relaxing his features, with a laugh, said: "I have a job for you." It was William Hodson. I had met him in India, but not since the days of his celebrity; and the joke about the "job" was in reference to years before, when I was his fag [1] at Rugby, and had to brush his study out, and make his coffee, by the time he came back from first lesson. Besides this relation, I had known him also in family circles, for his Archdeacon father belonged to a school of religionists, amongst whom my

[1] This was my second "situation." I had previously been valet to Dr. Gell, Bishop of Madras, on whom be peace!

people also took their part. Willie Hodson of the yellow hair—not great in cricket or football, but distinguished for running and athletic feats of endurance—was a soldier almost by an afterthought, for he had to get into the army through the Jersey Militia on account of age, finding his true throne at last on an Irregular Cavalry saddle. He had been wounded not long before, and the sleeve had been cut out of the blue, braided coat, to get his arm loose; and the "job" now was for me to have it sewn on for him by the time he returned. It was sewn on; but he never returned, and did not require the coat.

I do not know how it was, but there seemed a sort of understanding that something should be said between Hodson and myself about a certain event. Somehow, it occurred to both that the door should be shut for that purpose, and that he should sit down and tell me—as he began to do at once—how the Princes had been killed at Delhi. I had always wished, and wish now, that the action had never taken place; but I must bear testimony to the fact that Hodson spoke of the circumstance with no bitterness at what had been said in censure of it, and with no harshness or bravado, but in a calm, argumentative tone, certainly producing the impression that, rightly or wrongly, he had convinced himself that a stern political necessity existed at the moment for striking in such a manner as to cause a sudden and lasting terror. There I leave the matter of the Princes of Delhi. Hodson was then close to the end of his career; and after his death he was injudiciously held up as a notable specimen of a type of soldier he could not, and did not, pretend to emulate. But there are grades between Philip Sidney and Trenck, and if he bore an indistinct likeness to the first, I must say I think he should not have been compared to the second. I thought that morning's visit was a renewal of our old friendship. I was mistaken. I supposed it was a greeting; it was really a farewell.

A sign of altered times was the approach of persons with other aims than war, and other calls than those of duty.

Beato, of photographic celebrity, turned up—he who had made a reputation during the Crimean campaign; and, with others, came a French doctor, whom I had known at Agra. Into what shelter Dr. Sganerelle had flown during the Mutiny I do not know; but here he was, as sweet as ever on his theory for the cure of Asiatic cholera. He was a man of considerable knowledge, had seen many parts of the world, and seemed never to grow cold in his belief that cholera might eventually be stamped out, and that, in the meantime, cures could be effected with safety and certainty by means of the Sganarelle bath.

We talk of Asiatic cholera, and the disease has taken its place as one of the terrors of India, but native physicians attribute it to the English. It appeared, at any rate, in the form now associated with it, during one of Lord Hastings' wars; and an argumentative Bengalee might perhaps pen an essay on the inquiry, whether Shakspeare and patent leather boots were real benefits, when accompanied by brandy and cholera-morbus. The French medico, whom I distinguish as Dr. Sganarelle—for, like that worthy in *Le Médecin Volant*, he could boast, *J'ai des talents particuliers —j'ai des secrets*—had made up his mind, from historical researches into the disease, that cholera took its birth in a particular city, and was annually renewed and invigorated from its native place, travelling, as he considered he could trace, from it, as from a centre, in various directions. This city was Hyderabad, in the Deccan; and his proposal for the abolition of cholera was the complete sanitation of that metropolis. In addition to this master notion, Sganarelle had plans of his own for dealing with individual cases of the disease. He put the patient into a tin bath, fitting as nearly as might be to the human frame, in a semi-recumbent position, and boiled the mischief out.

Joseph, as steward of our large and irregular household, was becoming rather a personage. All travellers and visitors became acquainted with him, and laughed at his quaint and racy English. He has been sketched by no less a pen than that of Dr. Russell. Though very lean and old, Joseph was wonderfully tough; but his ancient blood required a little warming, and I observed that he took port wine for the purpose. As this stimulant was not used at the table, I asked him where he got it, and he replied, with much simplicity: "I have a friend in the Commissariat; I give him some of your tea, and he gives me Government wine." This arrangement, if open to some remark from the moral point of view, seemed to work well, and was only put an end to by the common severances of time.

The position of Joseph made him much sought after by some of his own compeers; and on one occasion, wishing to speak to him in the evening, I found him forming one of a small theological symposium, to whose discussions I thought myself entitled to listen for a short time at an open door. There was a visitor present, who claimed for himself the sobriquet of the Worm of the Bible, "for," said he, "if modesty requires that I should submit to comparison with an insignificant creeping thing, still I am such a worm as has fed on the sacred pages, till my substance, as it were, has become one with the Scriptures themselves." Joseph treated these subtleties with levity, and remarked that far from conceding such a title to his friend, he believed that the simplest hermeneutic difficulty would pose him. To this the Worm replied, there was no question Joseph could put which would not meet with an immediate answer. And Joseph, with severe dignity, said, "Then explain why Rachel weeping for her children would not be comforted." The Worm replied that there was no such passage in existence, and that the propounder of the question was demeaning himself by unsuitable frivolity. Joseph, with angry determination, sent for a Testament, and read the passage out, glaring at his adversary with not undeserved indignation. The Worm attempted to create a diversion by satire, and remarked that the company were awaiting, with some impatience, Joseph's own exegesis. "No," said Joseph, "the company will not be gratified; it is quite enough for this evening that you should have been completely defeated, and I shall not take out the interpretation till a future occasion."

A familiar figure in those days was that of Paterson Saunders, senior—so called in connection with a stout man of the same name, living Jounpore way, a cousin I fancy. I had known him at Agra, when he was conducting the *Messenger* at that place. He was a younger brother of the well-known J. O. B. Saunders, and was a man of a singularly fine character. He had been, when young, in South America, and knew Spanish well, which had earned for him the name of the Don. If he had been born in Elizabeth's days he would have gone forth and fought those with whom he had only traded, and would have helped to win some strange land for the British Crown. As it was, he was always looking for Eldorado. "Four lacs and member for Fife," was the ambitious programme, which he did not, however, fulfil. An upright, wiry man, with hanging grey locks, a fine seat on a horse, and a manly bearing. He was too ungirt for these latter days, and belonged to freer, more reckless, and more jovial habitudes; but he had a true chivalric spirit, a clear head, and wielded, moreover, a picturesque pen. He was often with us, galloping up to the house in the morning, and indeed occasionally riding gently from room to room on the handsome nag he had taught to trust his hand.

> "If we fell, we e'en gat up agen,
> And sae will we yet."

—a favourite refrain with him. How the old songs ring in one's ears, when the singers have long been silent!

The large body of troops that escaped by Calpee gave anxiety from time to time, and it was thought advisable, occasionally, to show troops in the part of the district lying near the river, and opposite to where they were posted in some force. Sir John Inglis had sent out a small column before the Lucknow operations began; and I accompanied it for a day or two. Mowbray Thomson was there, too. Part of the Force was the 34th Queen's Regiment. It was very pleasant to me to be with this corps, my uncle having served in it many years, and having given an account of some of its adventures in Spain, in his "Recollections of the Peninsular," a book which, in its day, had a great sale. The Connaught Rangers had asked Thomson to do them a little service. They had lost a young officer at the Battle of the Bridge, under Windham, and they had never found his body; he was believed to have fallen into a well. Thomson had promised to try and find out what had become of the body. So, as we rode home, we stopped at a village near, and asked some questions. The peasants do not like such subjects, and answered in the shuffling way they employ when they do not want to answer. But, at last, we found there was a well on the plain near, which was not used; and we got some coolies and went there. We sat waiting whilst the men descended with ropes, and at last they brought the poor fellow up. His name was Day. He must have been standing on the edge of the well to look ahead, when a round-shot caught him, and down he went. It was probably a chilly morning, and he had slipped on a mackintosh. His watch was there, and other little personal equipments, and his rings still encircled the bony fingers. We had him reverently laid on a charpoy and covered him up; and it was a consolation to his fellow-officers to place him in a grave, and to have the last words of hope read over him.[1]

Some little time before the troops were beginning to come back from Lucknow, I received confidential orders that I was to prepare to lithograph a certain document in an absolutely secret way. The paper had been, I think, in General Outram's hands, and had received some modifications on his own responsibility. I found that Umurnath, the Brahmin Tuhsildar, had been accustomed to write on stone, and did it clearly and well. There was a native in the city

[1] Mowbray Thomson went out again with Colonel G. V. Maxwell's detachment and Talbot's guns, and was wounded. See his "Story of Cawnpore."

who possessed a press, and I sent word to him that I was coming down to his house about nine at night, and that he must place his materials and the two workmen, the roller, and the pressman, at my disposal. These two could neither read nor write. So, after dinner, instead of going to my room, I popped into a carriage with Umurnath—no easy task—for the Brahmin required the greater part of a palkee-garee, and we went to the printer's house. Of course we sent him to bed, and locked ourselves in a room with the roller and the pressman. Then out I came with the document, and Umurnath [1] sat down to write it on the stone. It took a long time, and the workmen were very lazy and did not like staying; but, of course, no excuses could be taken, and after midnight we got all the copies safely pulled off and wrapped up—the stone cleansed from the writing, and all traces of our work removed. Then home; the packet of papers entrusted to the hand that was to receive them—and the task was over. This was Lord Canning's celebrated Proclamation, as slightly altered by Outram—a document which his lordship's apologists consider to have been right in substance, if rather injudiciously expressed. Col. Barrow was especially entrusted with its explanation, and it can scarcely be said to have retarded the pacification of the

1 When I returned to India, after furlough, in 1863, I found Pundit Umurnath a Deputy-Collector. His health, however, had failed. Extreme obesity brought on disease his native physicians were unable to deal with. He knew he was dying, and came to Mirzapur, to bid good-bye. When we were parting, he said, "You will not see me again, but when I am gone, you will know I had not forgotten the objects I was interested in." He left most of what money he possessed for educational purposes. The Government lost in him a very valuable servant.

province. Its Parliamentary effects, leading to Lord Ellenborough's explosion and subsequent resignation, are well known.

The days at Duncan's Hotel were drawing to a close. Dr. Russell has narrated how we cured him of his dysentery; and two of the last figures remembered are those of Sir Thomas Franks, with his fine person and his animated—nay, electrical—conversation, and the tall, manly frame of the lamented Venables.

X

THE NUWAB'S HOUSE

As the district was now pretty well in British occupation, business increased naturally, and we required fixed and spacious premises, for office accommodation. A large confiscated native house was chosen for Cutcherry, and a bungalow opposite for our head-quarters. A family who had made large sums of money at Lucknow in the old days had got sufficiently over the border to secure their property by settling at Cawnpore, and lived there, enjoying their wealth, and the rank they had received at the Oudh capital. There were three brothers, all Nuwabs, and two of them had undoubtedly joined the Nana; whilst, with regard to the third, who was called the Nunha Nuwab, or little Nuwab, some believed in his loyalty, and some did not.[1] He was not comfortable, however, at Cawnpore; and left India to reside at Mecca, a year or so after the Mutiny. Our bungalow belonged to one of the rebellious brothers, Bakur Ali, and when disencumbered of walls intended to seclude the women, was very nice, some of the ceilings

---

[1] Kaye has, I think, overrated his influence. I never heard of him that he was regarded as a leader by any section of his townsmen.

being painted, after the native fashion, the colouring effective, though the drawing, of course, was rude.

Before our move we had to make arrangements for receiving Jung Bahadur, who was on his way from Lucknow to Allahabad. The Savada Kotee, which played a well-known part in the Mutiny, was assigned to him. He arrived on horseback, and was met by a kind of procession: the Commanding Officer, and Douglas Forsyth—who was at Cawnpore, overlooking the Nana's papers—and other officials being present. The Prince had a spare, active figure, unwearied as yet by his years or his habits; but the face was very Goorkha, with the low brow, squab nose, and pointed eyebrows of his race. He wore goggles, too, partly for ornament, I expect, for he must have been well-accustomed to the sun. I sent him a carriage and some sowars; and on leaving he had a polite note written, saying he had been very comfortable.

There was at length a clergyman at Cawnpore, and an excellent one he was, named Moore. He and his wife received Sir William Peel into their house, and nursed him tenderly during his terrible illness—confluent small pox—till he succumbed. Our Baptist friend, Mr. Gregson, was therefore at liberty to move up to Agra. He had, I believe, contributed annals of the Mutiny to a leading Nonconformist journal in London, and was a man of intellect, and singularly free from sectarian prejudice.

Father Conti, also, though not a chaplain, held on for a time. His cheerful face always lighted up at a visit. He would be found smoking a hookah, and reading up, in case of possible controversies, Cobbett's "History of the Reformation."[1] A very genuine character, with much of the simplicity of the agricultural class in Italy.

We had scarcely got into our new quarters when the capture of Calpee took place. It was the height of the hot weather, and the sufferings of the soldiers must have been very great. Two of my coadjutors were out: Willock with a detachment watching the river, and James Power with Maxwell's Force that co-operated with Sir Hugh Rose, from the northern bank of the Jumna. Of course, the clearing-out of the rebels made a great difference, and materially strengthened all authority. By the time the cold weather arrived, we were able to camp out in the district; and it was, of course, desirable we should show our faces. But it was deemed better to display some little capability of enforcing what was thought right, in case of necessity, and so, this year, my movements were accompanied by some hundred or more of the military police, and five-and-twenty sowars. The competition system had supplied me with two companions, Tracy and E. S. Robertson. The former was a very fine young man, with a most pleasant wit, to which he did great injustice. He walked through life, to use Gautier's phrase, like a Hungarian noble, with pearls sewn on to his boots, strewing them on the floor, regardless whether they were picked up or not. Robertson was an economist and John Stuart Millite; was understood to have a scheme in his portfolio for the improved representation of the people, and was

1 The *Saturday Review* said at this point, "Perhaps Burnet's?" But, no; it was not the time for library octavos. William Cobbett's work is little more than a large pamphlet, powerful, perverse, overheated, but mainly true.

always game for a discussion, either on finance or colonial policy. He wielded a very clever pen, and amongst the narratives of district troubles during the Mutiny, drawn up by the order of Government, the report upon the Futtehpore district was written by him, from facts and circumstances supplied by me.

It was early in December, and our camp was near Sheorajpore. One forenoon, when out with Robertson on an elephant, news was suddenly brought us from Bilhour that rebels had appeared on the Oudh side of the Ganges, and were forcing their way across, as it was understood, with a view of escaping across the Doab. A messenger was sent off at once to Brigadier Percy Herbert, and we all started for Bilhour. After Sir John Inglis had gone home, Brigadier William Campbell commanded at Cawnpore, an officer who had made a celebrated mull of the pursuit at Lucknow, but who in private life was very amusing and pleasant, and had in his day been one of the best gentleman flat-race riders in England. He, however, died in the later autumn, and was succeeded by Percy Herbert, brother of Lord Powys, and who had distinguished himself in the Crimea. Soon after reaching the Grand Trunk Road, I met a string of camels, accompanied by huge, dirty Cabulees, in their long chogas, their baggy pyjamas, thick matted hair, and with matchlocks in their hands. I asked if there was any disturbance up the road. They showed their white teeth—the only clean thing about them—and answered, "*Bulwa khoob chulta,*" or, in other words, "There is a pretty shindy." Fortunately, there was an officer named Sullivan, with a native levy, not far off, and some rough Cavalry called Towana horse, and we all went together to Bilhour, reaching it the same evening. We learnt that the person commanding the rebels was Firoze Shah. They had completed their landing, and had occupied the encamping ground a mile or so higher up. The people at Bilhour were very glad of protection, as they were afraid of being looted. Brigadier Herbert behaved with the greatest promptitude. He wrote to me :—

"CAWNPORE,
"*December* 6, 1858, 4 a.m.

"MY DEAR SHERER,—Your note arrived about an hour ago. I have telegraphed to Lucknow, Allahabad, and Calpee. I am sending 200 European Infantry up to Bilhour to reinforce you. I have about 200 Cavalry of sorts here. I shall move them up the road or across country according to what I hear. I shall communicate my movements to you as much as possible. Send me all information available. "PERCY HERBERT."

He put two companies of the 80th Regiment under Captain Hume into bullock-train waggons, and sent them straight up the Trunk Road; and, forming a small flying body of cavalry, made off post-haste for the Jumna, hoping to catch the rebels. Firoze Shah was off in the night; and the next morning, when the troops came, and we moved forward, we found the store-house burnt down, and some of the buildings at the encamping ground still smoking, the telegraph wire cut, and strewed on the ground. The officer commanding the English soldiers had to wait for further orders; but some of us rode to a neighbouring village to inquire what had happened there, and learnt that the last troopers had only just left the little street. Firoze Shah was gallantly met in the next district by Lieutenant Forbes, Mr. Hume and Captain Doyle, and harrassed, though not arrested. He managed to get across the Jumna just before Brigadier Herbert came up; but the effect of these prompt movements was very good, for it showed that rebels could no longer venture into our territory without pursuers springing up in every direction. Captain Hume received his instructions to pursue across country, and Robertson volunteered to show the roads and to interpret. They marched to Phaphoond in Etawah; but, hearing there of the skirmishes with Firoze Shah, and the Prince's escape across the Jumna, turned back. Lord Canning afterwards personally thanked Robertson. On coming back to the Trunk Road, I found Herbert Harington, who has been mentioned before, sitting in a waggon, mending the telegraph wire. These road duties were sometimes perilous. He went out once to mend a wire near Nawab Gunj, in Oudh, with a companion and one or two sowars. Irregular troopers were suddenly seen stealing along the road to get between the party and the Gunj gate-way. It was a case of galloping. Harington stuck his spurs into old Socrates, a favourite horse, and at last got ahead; but he heard the breathing of the troopers' horses at his croup. A minute or two more and the gateway was gained. But the pursuers caught up poor Vaughan, his companion, and cut him off his saddle with their sabres.[1]

[1] Harington's son, Lieutenant Henry Harington, was mortally wounded in the night attack at Murkanai, September 14, 1897. His father said of him, "He leaves behind him a track of only the sweetest memories."

The camping that winter was very delightful. There is, perhaps, no climate more perfect than that of the cold weather in the central districts of the North-West. The golden mornings; the sunny but pleasant noons; the balmy elastic evenings; and the country, though never striking, oftentimes agreeably diversified by mango groves and tanks, the vast peepul trees of villages, and temples rising amidst verdure, and the slender minars of mosques. Then the welcome baskets of vegetables from the station, and the newspapers and letters from home. There was sporting, too, of the less exciting sort. Some of my friends used to say of my shooting, that even Professor Freeman could bring against it no moral objection, as it amused myself, and did no harm to any living thing. Matters were not so bad, perhaps, really as this; but I confess to the easy diversion of one more fond of natural history than acquainted with woodcraft. There were partridges, and sand grouse, and rock pigeons, and teal, and wild ducks, and wild geese, and sometimes deer and neel-gai. We had a grand old Brahmin with us as shikaree. He must have been close upon seventy, but was a picture of health and activity, and astounding at walking or swimming, or any bodily exercise. He shocked the Hindoo servants by shooting a neel-gai, which they thought going too far, because the name means blue *cow;* but he bore them down with his Brahminical rank, and declared that it was only a deer, and a fit object of sport.

We had, as we travelled along, occasionally to investigate cases of crime, of which the perpetrators were absent, but of which it seemed desirable to make some record, whilst evidence was available. In a village, a mile or two out of

Cawnpore, the farmer and the village accountant were on bad terms. The latter functionary is called up-country the Putwaree, and is often of the writing, or Kayuth caste. If he be a weak man he is the slave of the farmer; if a strong-willed person, he often sides with the peasants against the farmer. In the village I am speaking of, the Putwaree aided the tenants against their landlord, and he, again, had sworn vengeance should the British authority ever pass away. The day the Nana attacked Wheeler's entrenchment, at the first gun the farmer set out to look for his foe. It is said that Henry IV. of France heard, in the night before his assassination, the footsteps of Ravaillac in the streets of Paris. One may imagine that the trembling Putwaree, who had hidden for some days in his house, had heard a hundred times the farmer's dreadful step. This day it reached his door. The poor wretch was dragged out, bound hand and foot, laid on a stone before the temple of Kalee outside the village, and his throat being cut, he was solemnly sacrificed to the goddess.[1] It is gratifying to think that, on the whole, the British name was associated as a synonym with law. My moonshee told me that during the Mutiny he was living in a house in Bijnour, and heard his next-door neighbour quarrelling with his wife. During

[1] This anecdote seems to point to exceptional barbarity. And such cases, naturally, could not often occur. But it must be remembered that our nineteenth century civilisation, as it affects provincial life in India, is only a veneer over an older civilisation actuated by principles widely different from ours. Material advancement may outrun moral progress. The ancient Greeks were, in a sense, highly civilised. We still take them as our models in literature and art. But what were their views about slavery;—what their sentiments towards enemies? not to touch on some very painful features in their social life.

the misunderstanding the husband said: "You had better be careful; there are no British now, and no reason exists why I should not break your head and throw you into a well." The lady took the political crisis into consideration, and became silent.

Amongst the spoils which Henry Willock had brought in from the district was a pair of huge kettle-drums, which were duly advertised as confiscated property, but naturally did not command an easy sale. At one village I visited, a Goshain sent word he should be much obliged if I would call on him, explaining that he was prevented calling on me by a vow never to leave the storey of the house where he sat. So I went to him, and found a temple, with trees overshadowing it, surrounded by a court. The shrine was upstairs, on what we should call the first floor, and the Goshain was seated in a little chamber by its side. Dressed in saffron-dyed clothes, he looked venerable enough, with his iron-grey hair and ample beard. He delighted in his present quarters as the abode of miracle—for a peepul tree was growing out of the earthen floor of this upper storey, which he held to be altogether out of nature. He had only been for a year or two at the elevation he had chosen, and seemed pleased to refer to the occasion when he carried out his intention of permanently ascending. He described how he had walked round the village, for it was the place where he was born, and each hut and every turning were familiar, then put his foot resolutely on the first step, to descend no more till he should be brought down a dead body. He told me how the chamber where he sat had been filled, once during the disturbances, with soldiers, and how he feared he might have been dragged below. But no! The Deotar protected him. And now came the point of the interview. The kettle-drums! Willock's booty had come from this shrine, and the votary pined for his kettle-drums. No one accused the devotee of having been mixed up with the rebels, and it was a pleasure to be able to gratify him in so simple and inexpensive a way. He was allowed his kettle-drums. I had often before wondered what they could be, and I found they were used to announce service at the shrine. Many of the Mussulman fukeers were employed by the rebels as spies, and sometimes as Ghazees or desperadoes, who would rush on death, sustained by the hope of that reward which is thought to be in store for those who fall for Islam. But it was, of course, impossible to explain to T. Atkins the distinctions in devotional life, and one felt sorry for Hindoo saints who were sincere. If they had really given up the world, and having made up their minds that the phenomena surrounding them were Maya, or as Lecomte de Lisle calls them, "*L'unique l'eternelle et sainte Illusion*"—had fixed their thoughts on the Supreme essence—it was rather hard to be suddenly ordered by an apparition in a red coat to "Come out o' that," and to be kicked off their mats as the rascally clergy of the country. At Bithoor, the Nana's place, there was a saint, half visionary, half mountebank, who sat on a board on the top of a high pole, and passed his time between prayer and tying his legs in a knot round his neck. Whether the soldiers thought this new Simon Stylites an entertainment or not, I cannot say; but he escaped all difficulties, and we found him on his airy perch, during the winter of 1858, as acrobatic and spiritual as ever.

Some years after the Mutiny was concluded, and when

time was beginning, in a measure, to efface its events from the memories of men, I met an Eurasian gentleman of much ability, who had been Deputy-Collector with me, in the time the description of which is now drawing to a close. I asked him how he liked his station, and he replied: "Very much. The duties are not heavy, I am content and comfortable; but," he added, with a faint smile, "it is not like the golden days of Cawnpore." I felt a slight chill at my heart, and thought within myself, I hope he only means happy by "golden." For, of course, on the gradual restoration of order there were two openings for corruption —first, it was difficult to get native employées of whose antecedents one had any knowledge; and next, accounts and lists and checks were all out of gear, and there was a great deal of confiscated property; and, moreover, no end of people about with ready money in exchange for recommendations and good words. A little incident impressed upon me the extreme caution that was necessary to avoid a bad name, as also how prevalent the belief was in lax morality.

The Queen's Proclamation was read on the 1st of November, 1858. There were no especial circumstances attending its promulgation at Cawnpore; there was a parade, a sufficient but not remarkable collection of natives, and the senior civilian, Mr. Batten, the Judge, read the document out from a carriage. Not far from the station was the village of a Rajpoot, named Goolab Singh, who was understood to have joined Tantia Topee in the attack on the entrenchment. He had fled across the Jumna, and hearing that the Proclamation was going to be issued, out of mere bravado crossed over into the Cawnpore district, on the morning of the 31st October. But the part where he entered was in the jurisdiction of a hot-headed Mussulman Thanadar, who determined to arrest him, as he was quite justified in doing, for the amnesty merely extended to those who came in under the Proclamation, and was on that day only *in posse*. The Mahomedan surrounded the house, and the door was burst open, and he ordered the constables to enter. But no one ventured to face the old Rajpoot, who was sitting on a charpoy. The Thanadar drew his sword and rushed in. Goolab Singh shot him with a revolver, and the Mahomedan, although mortally wounded, with a last effort ran the Rajpoot through. They both fell dead in the court. The story was so romantic that I was anxious to get the revolver; and though I had endeavoured to avoid being mixed up in any way with confiscated property, I asked the Nazir to buy this article in for me. It was knocked down at Rs40 (£4), which was really quite as much as it was worth. When I was leaving Cawnpore, a native gentleman asked if he might say what he thought of me, without giving offence. To see ourselves as others see us is a gift desired of the gods, and I replied: "Certainly." He said: "I have watched you very carefully, and I believe you to be an honest gentleman. You have had many opportunities, and you have only stolen one thing—the pistol of Goolab Singh!" And as if this wretched weapon carried a fatality with it, it had already subjected me to an insulting importunity, for in one of our camping expeditions the son of Goolab Singh accompanied us, paying his compliments each day, till at last he thought he was favourably viewed enough to address me in a very coaxing tone: "I say, Sahib, give me back *my* pistol!"

But if the times were lax, and the agency rough, the plan of appointing Zemindars as *pro tem* Tuhsildars answered very well; and in one case, Kindur Singh, who was hereditary chief of his clan, and was educated enough to write Persian, not only kept his neighbourhood perfectly quiet, but exhibited considerable talents for business. An old gentleman in horn spectacles, and his teeth tied in his mouth apparently with soda water bottle wires, he did not look as if he could control a clan; but his influence was very great. I was the means, through representation of his worth, of considerably enlarging his estates; but he did not very long enjoy his prosperity, for he was killed in a railway accident, actually in the station-yard of Cawnpore.

Before the winter ended we had a guest in Mr. James Wilson, the Finance Minister, who came up to make local inquiries as to a tax on tobacco, and other projects. He was a shaggy-browed Scotchman, of middle height, and sturdy enough frame, very pleasant in conversation, though occasionally subject to going off suddenly into the Hamburg currency, and kindred topics, whither the inexperts went floundering after him. As he wished to write overland dispatches, I had prepared a tent looking over the terraces of the garden; the flowers, and then the pomegranates and oranges, and at last, through breaks in the boughs of the neems and Dalbergias, the river Ganges. I thought the sunshiny vistas might inspire him with a few poetic thoughts; but when I went in to see if the post was ready, I found he had closed up the side towards the landscape. I suppose, as the painter Fuseli said was the case with himself, "Nature put him out."

People pride themselves on comparatively unimportant

achievements. Théophile Gautier was more proud of the blow from his fist which, at the opening of the *Château Rouge*, marked, on the new "Turk's Head," 582 pounds, than he was of his poetry and romances.

In humbler life I pin my celebrity to "The Fine."

The City of Cawnpore was mulcted £30,000 (three lacs of rupees) for its too ready acceptance of the Nana's occupation; and this sum was successfully realised without an appeal. A protest, indeed, reached me from a goldsmith and banker, who claimed not to have been a regular resident, and he had up a solicitor from Calcutta to fight the matter out. But this functionary, who was an exeellent fellow, wrote to ask me what I should do if his client did *not* pay. In a moment of inspiration I replied: "I should resort to the usual processes for recovering revenue." One of these was personal arrest, and the protest was therefore withdrawn. And thus Apollo came to my aid.

The spring wore away, and then the summer, and one Sunday morning I was starting for the house of my kind friend, Dr. Tresidder, who had said: "Come to a quiet room which I will give you, where you may write up your letters, free from interruption," when, on sitting down in the carriage, I found myself as cold as death, teeth chattering, and every limb trembling, which state of things gave place to burning heat by the time I reached the doctor's. In about three weeks' time I was able to leave this kindly home, after a jungle fever, which troubled me in many ways for about a quarter of a century. It was very provoking, for Lord Canning was just coming at the commencement of the cold season to hold a Durbar, and there were all sorts of arrangements to be made for the native Princes but everyone helped, and matters were got into good trim.

The Durbar, when it came off, was not a splendid one; but the occasion was suitable enough, and it was desirable that the country should see that pageants could now be resumed, as well as the ordinary business of the day. Willoughby Osborne brought his Rewar Raja, a fine, tall man; and the good old Ishree, Maharaja of Benares, was there; and Sir Richmond Shakspeare escorted Punna, Bettiah, and some of the minor monarchs of mid India. There was rather a droll incident at the Durbar itself. One of the small Rajpoot chieftains had brought an old grey and toothless courtier, who had got himself up in a ferociously warlike manner, and carried a portentous sword of the pantomimic scimitar description, such as I have seen handled by the late Mr. W. H. Payne, when with terrific moustache and a turban of many-coloured folds, he enacted the part of the cruel Sultan in a Christmas piece. The old gentleman brought this heart-rending weapon to be touched by Lord Canning, and then in a loud voice began telling him that if his enemies ever gave him any trouble, he had only to say the word and this sword should be drawn in his defence. He had a great deal more to state, but fell at last into the hands of the Masters of the Ceremonies, and was hustled out of the presence, not, however, before he had quite upset Lord Canning's gravity, who held out for some time, but at last burst into uncontrolled laughter.

When the Viceroy moved up-country, the Commissioner and myself accompanied the camp to the limit of the district. Fortune had been favourable again in the matter of a Commissioner, for the kindly and able Cuthbert Thornhill held the post. The last morning, he and I got up early, and rode out to a small roadside police-station, just on the edge of the Cawnpore jurisdiction. The motley groups accompanying a large encampment passed us, as we sat on a charpoy under the little verandah, till at last the highway was quite clear. Then a cloud of dust appeared far off, which grew into a carriage with outriders, and Lord and Lady Canning came up. The Countess had been, as is well-known, in her day, a *Keepsake* beauty, and was engraved with her sister as "Hermia" and "Helena," when Mr. Charles Heath employed his *burin* in introducing gracious faces to the public. She still retained her good looks, and was noted for the ease and affability of her manner. There was to my mind always something tragic about Lord Canning's countenance. The brow was as fine almost as that of his father; but the lower part of his face was weak. There was, too, a look about him of Hamlet distraction: that he, the muser, should have fallen on days demanding masterly action:

> "The time is out of joint, O cursed spite,
> That ever I was born to set it right."

He is not a very distinct figure in the eulogies of Sir John Kaye, whilst, on the other hand, his letters seem to disprove some of the opinions of his opponents. Perhaps, as time wears on, and all temptations to partisanship are removed, we may arrive at a delineation which will present to us the man as he really was.

Thornhill, who had considerable talents in design, had made himself very useful—indeed indispensable—in settling the plans for the new town at Allahabad, and Lord Canning spoke very warmly to him in acknowledgment; and then, on her part, Lady Canning added some kind words. Thornhill was, of course, gratified, and his face was bright as we took off our hats and the carriage moved away. It was an interview of doomed people; for, with the exception of myself, who may be held to have been a bystander, within a very short time they had all departed. There is no Earldom of Canning now, and the property is held in the family of Clanricarde. Near the river Hooghly, in the beautiful park of Barrackpore, the lady is resting; and the very title of the noble house from which she sprang—Stuart de Rothesay—is extinct. The remains of poor Thornhill were committed to the waters of the tropic sea. Of the Earl Canning, however, a lasting memorial remains in Westminster Abbey, in the shape of one of the finest statues of modern times. Foley certainly surpassed himself in its execution. All that was poor and less worthy is suppressed, whilst the head denotes that intellectual superiority which undoubtedly existed. The pose is commanding and dignified; and the nervous gathering up of the senatorial robe in the full-veined hand incomparable.

Our household arrangements had undergone some modification, for Badul Khan, who had sorrowfully bid us farewell the night before we left Futtehpore, suddenly appeared one morning with a cart containing his goods and chattels, including his wife, and claimed the direction of *cuisine* as an old-standing right.

Joseph was not very unwilling to resign, for accounts were always burdensome to him, and we had found it necessary to audit them with more precision than was altogether pleasant to his feelings. The actual writer of the house accounts was a little old cripple, who rode up daily for the purpose, on the most unfed of ponies. He professed to know English, but was occasionally very uncertain, and articles of consumption appeared of which no explanation seemed possible. One was a "Windquick," an implement whose origin and uses remained obscure, but as it only cost twopence, the item was passed without remonstrance. The scribe loved to insert his own name at an erasure, or alongside of his Total, and generally with qualifications calculated to move pity, such as "*lame, with very children!*" Joseph retained an apartment on the premises, where he received his friends.[1]

One morning, Joseph brought a gentleman whom he said he wished to introduce to me, and a ginger-whiskered Englishman, past middle age, of moderate stature, walked in, whom I discovered to be the celebrated Mr. De Russet, celebrated, at least, to those who have read "The Private Life of an Eastern King." For he was the very barber to whose skill the elaborate locks of Nusr-ood-Deen-Hyder bear testimony in the effigies of him to be seen in the Moosa Bagh at Lucknow. In later interviews he declared to me that the book was a pure romance; but he was too interested a party to be received as an impartial critic. One thing he stoutly declared, which I thought not unlikely, namely, that the conversations between the King and the librarian were purely imaginary; in proof of which, he urged that the King knew only two or three words of

[1] Poor old Joseph died at Allahabad in 1873.—*R.I.P.*

English, whilst the librarian was equally ignorant of Hindoostanee. All traces of fast life had disappeared, if they ever existed, from the appearance of Mr. De Russet, and he bore every aspect of a quiet, well-to-do tradesman. As the winter wore on, Mr. George Edmonstone appeared, and inspected the institutions of Cawnpore. His secretary, Couper, was an old Haileybury friend, and it was pleasant, in the altered circumstances, to recall former days, when we were young, and excusably (or inexcusably) foolish. He succeeded to his father's baronetcy, and became Civil Commissioner of Oudh, and afterwards followed Mr. Edmonstone as Lieutenant-Governor of the North-West Provinces. But he always remained the simple and cordial comrade of old, retaining his love of those quips and jokes which help to brighten the hours, and are not unpleasant to recall, even when their mild effervescence has finally subsided.

It was in this winter, 1859-60, that the Nana died in the jungles of Nepaul. The event was marked by the passage through Oudh of a body of people who had been in attendance on Doondoo Punt, or supported by him. At the same time, too, Jowala Purshad was captured. He, of course, was very strictly guarded, and sent to Cawnpore, a close prisoner. But most of the others were merely pushed on, under temporary arrest, towards Bithoor and other places they wished to reach. Several were in custody with us at Cawnpore, and very disagreeable charges they were, for their blood was so corrupted by the malaria of the forest, that it was most difficult to keep them alive. Carts were ordered to the railway when they arrived, but one man died on the way from the station; another, striking his ankle against the threshold of the lock-up, had such an angry swelling that he was not strong enough to sustain it, and succumbed.

The personal barber of the Nana was in this worn-out company. I regret to say he was very faithless and ungrateful to his patron. He never mentioned his name without an abusive expression, for which "blackguard" must inadequately serve. We subjected this attendant to a catechism something as follows:—

"You shaved the Nana?"

"Shaved whom?"

"The Nana."

"Oh, the Nana (blackguard!). Yes, I shaved the Nana (blackguard!)."

"How often a week?"

"Twice a week (blackguard!)."

"And now he does not require shaving. Do you think he is really dead?"

"Oh, he's dead enough (blackguard!), and a good thing, too (blackguard!)."

Alas! for human nature.

It has once or twice, since those days, been doubted whether the Nana did die, as reported. I think the doubts were unreasonable. When Jowala Purshad was in our lock-up, as his fate was quite certain, and escape impossible, I directed a modification of his fetters, which enabled him to eat with more convenience, and he was grateful. Moreover, he knew his sentence did not depend on me, and so he was not afraid, and answered readily when I spoke to him. He told me, if I remember his words rightly, that he was not present when the Nana died, but that he attended when the body was burned. He spoke apparently without intention to deceive, and I fully believed him.

And so the period which can properly be called the Mutiny time came to its close. Health had been injured by the severe jungle fever, and friends were kindly unanimous in saying that a holiday had been earned. So my father-in-law and myself—with a temerity only exceeded by that of the Government in accepting it—gave our joint security for what, in those days, was called the "Inefficient Balance," which at Cawnpore had risen, through unadjusted advances for military purposes, public works, and commissariat, to twenty-six lacs (£260,000) and I started by dâk-garee, through the long roadside avenues, till hill and valley were reached; and so through the jungles of Sherghatty to a railway station some hundred miles from Calcutta.

When I reached the metropolis, I found Harington living with Outram and Le Geyt, the latter being the legislative member for Bombay. The Indian Bayard, when I was driving in the carriage with him in the evening, with no especial claim to his confidence whatever, often spoke to me of passages in his career. The sense of his own celebrity never seemed to occur to him, and he talked about public events with the same simplicity with which on "the course," in the midst of all the fashionables, he would stop and chaffer, jokingly, about the price of "*Tupsee Much*," as the vendors of the renowned "mango fish" brought it along, fresh from the river. But it was not in the carriage, but at the house, and before several people, including the gaunt, talkative Chisholm Anstey, who was visiting Calcutta, that Outram began to speak of having postponed taking charge from Havelock till the Bailey Guard was reached. "It was a foolish thing," he said; "sentiment had obscured duty. Every man should carry out the task assigned to him. I do not know that I could not have got through the streets of Lucknow with less loss of life. At any rate, I ought to have tried what I could do." This plainly-expressed regret seemed to me to do his character as much credit as the mistaken but noble impulse which called it forth.

These days were before the Bill—brought in by Sir Charles Wood—"for the abolition of Sir Barnes Peacock," and I visited the Legislative Council, which was, just then, a partially popular assembly. The members stood up, behind their respective desks, and spoke, with more or less point and fluency. Mr. James Wilson, as an old House of Commons *habitué*, was enabled of course, in some degree, like Dr. Johnson's lion, "to ravage without resistance, and roar without reply."

But there was an exception. The pale, small man, who occupied the chair, was possessed of an infinitude of calm self-reliance, and even the great Economist himself was obliged to admit that there was no over-riding Sir Barnes. I was "accommodated" with a seat on the Bench, during the remarkable trial of the "forged will" (Government *v.* Shibkrishnu and Others), when one of the richest and most influental Baboos in Calcutta was transported to the Nâf river for fourteen years, and Dr. Crawford sentenced to eight years' penal servitude. At length the "mail-day" came, on which I was to start. Harington drove me down to breakfast, on the river bank, with the Master Attendant, and I was by him kindly put on board the steamship *Simla*.

APPENDIX

A FEW letters are added in this place, which either illustrate the narrative, or may perhaps interest, simply from the names subscribed to them.

I

The evening before I left Calcutta in 1860, Sir James Outram said to me at dinner:

"Did I ever mention your name in any dispatch?"

My reply was:

"I think not, sir, because I should have been sure to have had the fact told me, if I had not seen the notice myself."

He remarked that he had certainly meant to have done so.

The subject dropped. But the next morning, when I was leaving, Sir James came out of his room, in his dressing-gown, and presented me with the following letter, begging me to make any use of it I liked.

I have had it by me for many years, but have not shown it to any one, as I thought it too kindly expressed. Old age, however, removes these hesitations, and moreover, a highly distinguished man has put down, in the most popular book of 1897, a sentiment on this subject, which recommends itself to one's reason. "It is better," he says in effect, "to be thought egotistical than to seem ungrateful."

This, then, is a copy of the original which lies before me, in the Bayard's firm and clear handwriting.

"CALCUTTA,
"9th *April*, 1860.

"MY DEAR SHERER,—I cannot allow you to leave India without discharging a debt which I have long owed you, and which I ought not to have delayed till now to endeavour to repay.

"I am almost certain that in my writings to the Governor-General, Commander-in-Chief, or Mansfield, while at the Alum Bagh, after we were released from the Bailey Guard, I gratefully recorded how much Havelock and I, and, indeed, the whole Lucknow force, were indebted to you for your exertions in our aid, while you were chief civil functionary at Cawnpore, during the trying time of our advance from thence to Lucknow, during the period we were shut up there, and afterwards, while we maintained the Alum Bagh position.

"The cordiality with which you worked with Bruce and other military men, to aid us with supplies, carriage, and intelligence, was the more praiseworthy and remarkable from the fact that your functions and authority, as head of the Civil Department, were interfered with, and trenched upon, by Neill, Havelock, and myself, having conferred powers on Major Bruce quite unusual, and such as might well have excited the jealousy and indignation of most men, and would have discouraged, if not disinclined, most men from heartily working with the military. Yet, so far from your taking offence, or relaxing in your endeavours to aid us, you ever earnestly exerted your utmost influence in the district, and the most unwearied, unceasing, personal labours in our behalf. However little we may have said of it at this time, I can assure you, my dear Sherer, your hearty, cordial goodwill and friendly assistance were deeply felt by us all. I have often blamed myself for not having sent you an official acknowledgment of your services in aid of the Army at Lucknow, when I relinquished my command. I was then so overwhelmed with incessant calls on my attention that I overlooked it at the time; and the least I can now do is to express to you, in this private form, what I ought to have said officially, while yet I was in a position to address you officially.

"I wish you a pleasant voyage, and happy meeting with your family, with all my heart.

"Believe me,

"Very sincerely yours,

"J. OUTRAM."

II

GENERAL NEILL

ON HIS OWN MILITARY POLICE

"CAWNPORE,

"*27th August*, 1857.

"MY DEAR SHERER,—*If* we had the men—soldiers—to send out, and take military possession of the country, all would be well. Your police could then go out and be efficient; but as we have not the men, and the country is in the possession of the enemy, I may say, attempting to establish your police is not only useless, but risking the lives of men well-disposed to the state to no purpose. The murders and captures of your men at Sheorajpore and Bithoor prove this.[1]

"My idea is—it would be the height of cruelty, and very impolitic to risk any more men in the country to the north-west, and partly south of this, towards Calpee, until, by military force, the insurgents are put down.

"Having no soldiers to send out, the armed police, under military rule Bruce is getting together, is the best substitute. As regards your police between this and Allahabad, they have been most efficient, and it is wonderful they have stood. They ought to be supported by a detachment at Futtehpore, to be at the call of the civil power to act whenever insurgents may appear. It is trying these men very hard, and more to their credit that they stand to their posts with no military support to fall back upon between this and Allahabad.

"When the sanction of Government is requested [for his armed police], the reason why must be fully stated, as above. Most certainly the grounds for making the request will not be the inefficient state of the present police. I never intended such to be understood, for I consider your police, as far as it is established, quite efficient. What I did mean was, that no police was efficient in a country in possession of the enemy, where, as has occurred, your men have been overpowered and murdered by overwhelming

[1] There is a little confusion here about names. Bruce lost the post at Bithoor.—J. W. S.

numbers of armed men, against whom, poor, almost unarmed, men, they could not have the slightest chance.

"Believe me,

"Yours very sincerely,

"J. S. Neill."

III

General Havelock

A LOYAL FARMER

"Cantonment,
"15th *August*, 1857.

"My Dear Mr. Sherer,—Many thanks for the information. Kindly let a letter of thanks be written to Hur Deo Buksh in my name, for my signature. I shall be obliged if you will send a Moonshee to read it to me. Assure the Zemindar of the protection of the British Government, and ask him if he requires any aid.

"Yours very sincerely,

"H. Havelock."

IV

General Mansfield (afterwards Lord Sandhurst)

CURRENT WORK

"Camp Meeranki Serai,
"Futtehgurh District,
"29*th December*, 1857.

. . . .

"I beg you to consult freely with Brigadier Inglis on the necessity of following up what is now being done by the movable Column which has been ordered to be formed. The sooner it is in movement the better, according to His Excellency. Had you not better organise a Tosha Khana to receive all treasure which may be found? The Brigadier writes to inquire what is to be done with the treasure trove of Bithoor. The C in C can only suggest the transfer of it to you. Government says there is to be no prize. Until, therefore, another determination be come to on this point, H. E. rules that the soldiers should not be led into temptation by having to take care of it. I shall instruct Inglis in the same sense, by H. E.'s orders.

"Yours ever very truly,

"W. R. Mansfield."

V

From W. H. Russell, Esq. (now Sir William)

A SPECIMEN OF HIS AMUSING AND INTERESTING LETTERS, PRINTED BY HIS PERMISSION

"Headquarters, Ajuddiah,
"Near Churda,
"29*th December*, 1858.

"Most Excellent Beak,—Unfriendly silence tortures your friend. Pardon will be freely given, however, if reparation comes. And now to thank you for the old hoss, and to tell you that he and I suit each other exactly, and that I am very much obliged and indebted to you for procuring him for me. Do you wish to sell him, and if so, what is his price? The campaign is, I consider, quite over, though throats won't be safe, or guns silent, in India for some months to come. I am exceedingly perplexed with these people. They will neither fight nor submit, and one knows not where to have them. After much dodging, we, marching twenty miles a day, came up with a body, under Beni Madho, the Nana's general, some notorious Mussulman rebels, and the Churda Rajah, on the 26th. They had seven or eight guns, and opened *with grape* when we came within a mile of them, then bolted so fast that neither Cavalry nor Horse Artillery could do more than take six of their guns—all good ones—and kill about twelve of them. This was some four or five miles from Churda. They evacuated that fort, and came on here. We attacked them next day, and, after an hour or two of artillery, they fled from the fort, which is by far the best I have seen in India, leaving a great quantity of powder, six good guns, and lots of grain and food, behind them. Now we don't know where to go. Rowcroft has defeated Bala Bao at Toolseepore and taken the fort, and we expect to hear the Begum has surrendered to Grant. I have sent divers and several commissions to my long-suffering friend to execute. The parcels, guns, etc., of which I wrote, have been in the Cawnpore post office for months two. And so may the Saints have you in their holy keeping. "Yours as ever,

"W. H. Russell.

"Lord Clyde was thrown in the pursuit on 26th, and put out his shoulder. He is much shaken."

VI

The Nuwab of Banda

"Indore,

"20*th October*, 1859.

"Sir,—I take the present opportunity of addressing you in my behalf, feeling assured that my application will receive your favourable consideration, and beg to remind you of a verbal promise which you gave me when you were a guest at my house, that, if at any time you could forward my interests, you would do so.

"The time has now come when your influence, if exerted

in my favour, will greatly benefit me. Previous to the Mutiny I received a pension of four lacs of rupees, and held the territory of Banda, as a Malgoozar, for many years, but of which I have been deprived since 1857, and only receive, in lieu thereof, a small sum of forty thousand rupees annually.

"My object is, through your kind recommendation and influence with his Lordship, the Governor-General, to have my pension and Malgoozaree restored. I beg respectfully to tender you my best wishes for your future welfare, and assure you of my grateful acknowledgment for any service you may render me.

"Yours sincerely,

"ALI BUHADOOR, OF BANDA."

[The Nuwab had taken the field against the Government, and no private individual could interfere. I had never been officially connected with him. As an acquaintance, I sincerely pitied him. He died not long afterwards.]

VII

FROM A. H. LAYARD, ESQ., M.P. (AFTERWARDS SIR AUSTEN)

MOWBRAY THOMSON'S CLAIMS

"120 PICCADILLY,
"9*th August*, 1858.

"MY DEAR SIR,—When I was with you at Cawnpore you promised to send me a note of Lieutenant Thomson's service and sufferings. I expected for some time to receive that document, as I felt a very lively interest in the subject, and was most anxious to do anything in my power to obtain for Lieutenant Thomson some acknowledgment of his noble conduct. Not having heard from you, I drew up a short memorandum in a letter to Mangles, which he has submitted to his colleagues at the India Board, promising me to do all he could to obtain some recognition of Lieutenant Thomson's services. I do not know what may have been done, but I shall not lose any opportunity that may present itself of pushing the matter.

"If you could send me any documents, or any statement on the subject, and could suggest any mode of action, I should be very glad, indeed, to do more.

"I write to you because I would not have you think that I had forgotten my promise.

"I hope you have been quite well since I had the pleasure of seeing you. The late telegrams from India bring more cheering accounts of the state of things, and I sincerely hope that ere long you will restore the country to its original state of peace and security. I fear, however, that there will be much to do before such reforms will be made in our Indian Government as appear to me to be essentially necessary to our permanent occupation of India, with advantage to ourselves, and its inhabitants.

"I wish I could look forward to another visit to a country which interested me so deeply during my short residence in it.

"Pray remember me kindly to those gentlemen who may be with you, and who may not have forgotten me.

"Believe me,

"Yours very truly,

"A. H. LAYARD."

[General Mowbray Thomson, a hale and hearty veteran, remains still without honours or decorations of any kind. But people ask: "What can the War Office do after forty years?" The question does not seem difficult to answer. There is no statute of limitations, to use Col. Maude's words, in regard to the public gratitude. Neglect does not become less wounding by lapse of time, and the obligation to reward conspicuous merit in the Army never ceases till to bestow reward would be impossible. What can the War Office do after forty years? Retrieve a mistake, and without further delay, before it is too late. Major-General H. G. Delafosse has got the decoration of C.B.; he richly deserved it. But his success makes the case of Mowbray Thomson so much the stronger.]

VIII

From Lieut.-Col. Sir H. Havelock (afterwards Sir Henry Havelock-Allan)

CERTIFICATE

"London, W.,
"14 Kensington Park Gardens,
"1st *June*, 1860.

"My Dear Sir,—I have very great pleasure in sending you the certificate you desire, in duplicate (in case it should be so wanted), and on thin paper, as I presume it is for transmission overland.

"If it is not sufficiently distinct for your purpose, I shall be happy to amend it at your suggestion.

"Many thanks, indeed, for your kindness in carrying out my wishes as regards the old woman. I trust she has profited by your counsel, and kept clear of the harpies who were ready to ease her of her newly-gotten wealth.

"It will give me great pleasure if I can be of any further assistance in regard to your claims on the Government of India, and I beg you will not scruple to ask me for any attestation that may be necessary to establish facts concerning the hard days of 1857.

"Believe me,

"My dear sir,

"Yours very truly,

"H. M. HAVELOCK."

[I had only Mr. Chester's verbal order to accompany the Force to Cawnpore; nothing in writing whatever; and it occurred to me that I could not show (if ever it might be necessary) that I had any right to join in the expedition. So I wrote to Col. Havelock to ask him as late D.A. Adjutant-General to his father, to certify that I was attached to the Force. This he fully, perhaps too fully, did, stating that I was recognised by General Havelock as the senior civil officer representing the Government of India. I have given his whole letter under the idea that some who knew his firmness and determination might be pleased to see how courteous and considerate he could be, and that the strong, unpersuadable man, who came to a wild, sad end, could warmly interest himself about an old woman, a dependent of his family, for whom he had arranged a pension, and whom he had asked me to protect from designing relatives.]

IN MEMORIAM

It is sorrowful enough, in writing of the days to which this volume refers, to remember what ravages death then made amongst men who had passed their youth together, or had, at least, the pleasant tie of a common college. And now the long years have done their work, too, and we, who started from Haileybury some fifty or more years ago in such high spirits, are reduced to "a sadly altered few."

> "En partant du Golfe d'Otrante,
> Nous étions trente ;
> Mais en arrivant à Cadiz,
> Nous étions dix."

Last year a tablet was erected in the chapel of Haileybury College to the memory of those Indian civilians who met their end in the Mutiny time. The proposal to put up a memorial was warmly accepted by the New Haileybury authorities, and, now it is finished and in place, it has their equally warm approval. This state of feeling is extremely gratifying. I give the inscription, but do not know by whom it was written. I cannot but remark that it seems to me very appropriate, and to fulfil every requirement of sentiment and taste.